FO

MW00878089

EXPOSITIONS FROM GOD'S HOLY WORD

Researched, written, and published for you, this insightful book of eleven Bible expositions will become one you will want to read over and over. Its rich content will fill you with joy as the words seem to leap off the page and into your heart.

By: Gladys Goldsby Ford
Editor: Monique D. Wild
Cover Design By: Kharis Courtney

FOR HIS GLORY

Scripture quotations are from
the King James Version of the Bible.
All Greek and Hebrew definitions are
from the Strong's Exhaustive Concordance.

You are welcome to copy portions of this book.
However, no portion is to be reproduced and sold.

TABLE OF CONTENTS

DEDICATION

"For His Glory" is dedicated to the God who called this former-blasphemer out of darkness to walk in his marvelous light. (1st Peter 2:9)

Knowing that my heart was so hard that I would not allow a Bible in my house, he still mercifully drew me out of the world and into fellowship with him. What a glorious transition!

This has made me a debtor to all men. I must share the love of God and understanding of his word that he has imparted. I am not a theologian; I am just me trying to do my part.

ALSO

"Also" is one of the biggest little words in the entire Bible. It's a hinge word, sort of like a door hinge. The importance of this little-big word will be emphasized as we continue.

The prophet Isaiah is quoted over sixty-five times in the New Testament where his name is mentioned thirty times. His writings are far reaching and often eloquent. He wrote in an expressive vocabulary that engages the reader.

His prophesies are known for their consistent literal fulfillment. In Chapter 7:14, he wrote of Emmanuel being born of a virgin, and in 9:6-7 he wrote of the promised Messiah. He accurately foretold of Messiah's suffering and death in Chapter 53.

Jewish tradition names Amos, Isaiah's father, as King Uzziah's uncle. That relationship made Isaiah a member of the royal family and gave him access to the king. His sixty year prophetic ministry in and around Jerusalem during the reign of four kings continued following the death of King Uzziah in 739 B.C.

Judgment had fallen on King Uzziah following his overstepping God-set boundaries which resulted in his becoming leprous seven years prior to his death. During this time and following his death, his son reigned in his stead.

2ⁿᵈ Chronicles 26:15 (Speaking of Uzziah) ... And his name was spread far abroad; for he was marvelously helped, till he was strong. **But** when he was strong, his heart was lifted up to his destruction; for he transgressed against the Lord, his God, and went into the temple of the Lord to burn incense upon the altar of incense.

No other Bible book begins with a vision. Thank God he had a vision - a vision of God's holiness. In the first five chapters, Isaiah displays the heart wrenching sadness of God over his sin-laden people as he pleaded with feeble-fallen-finite man to forsake sin. He pronounced six woes against backslidden Israel warning of the coming judgment of God caused by religious apostasy and moral corruption. Blind and deaf Israel did not heed the heartbroken Isaiah's call for national repentance.

With that being said, let's look at that little-big word **"also"** that changed his focus and may change yours too!

6:1 In the year that King Uzziah died, I saw **also** the Lord sitting upon a throne, high and lifted up, and his train filled the temple.

He saw the Lord sitting on a throne. He was not having a panic attack or pacing in his throne room. In all of your dilemma, how do you see God? He is God alone and he is God enough.

This is an often quoted scripture, and, is unfortunately often misquoted. It may be that when we are quoting a favorite scripture we leap over a little-big word. Many times the word **"also"** is left out or blurred over in our quoting this verse and its significance is lost.

Yes, he saw his nation under judgment, and yes, he saw the gross sin. But his entire perspective changed when he saw **"also** the Lord."

You may see your child or grandchild wearing more ink than a small town newspaper, you may see the world racing toward judgment, and you may see many things you'd rather not see. You are not in denial. But you may have become weary as they became your focus.

Like Isaiah, we need to see something else **"also."** Whatever we focus on is magnified. We are to set our affections on things above and magnify God alone.

> **Psalm 34:3** (written by King David) Oh, magnify the Lord with me, and let us exalt his name together.

I want to encourage you to focus on him with others who are doing the same.

Later, in chapter six, his attention was diverted after seeing God upon his throne, Isaiah's cry became, "Woe is me!" When we see God as he is we then can see ourselves as we are, and our cry becomes, "Woe is me!"

Isaiah 43:10 Ye are my witnesses, saith the Lord, and my servant whom I have <u>chosen</u>, that ye may <u>know and believe</u> me, and <u>understand</u> that I am he; before me there was no God formed, neither shall there be after me.

What a privilege! They were chosen by God to know him, to believe him, and to understand him.

Here is Jesus' response to a Pharisee lawyer who asked which the greatest commandment was:

> **Matthew 22:37-40** Jesus said unto him, Thou shalt love the Lord, thy God, with all thy heart, and with all thy soul, and with all thy mind. This is the first and great commandment. And the second is like it, Thou shalt love thy neighbor as thyself. On these two commandments hang (hinge) all the law and the prophets.

"Also" is said to be a hinge word. Our present and future contentment can hinge on this one word. "Also" is plural and means in addition too. You are not denying the sin-sick world we live in; but, like Isaiah, you must see something else **also**.

Remember that in **6:1**, he wrote, "I saw **also** the Lord ..."
And in **6:8** there is another important **also**:
"**Also** I heard the voice of the Lord ..."

Telling others what we have seen and heard from the Lord is a primary assignment of all believers.

Acts 22:14-15 (The Lord sent Ananias to pray for Saul (Paul), And he said, The God of our fathers hath chosen thee, that thou shouldest know his will, and see that Just One, and shouldest hear the voice of his mouth. For thou shalt be his witness unto all men of what thou hast <u>seen and heard</u>.

Proverbs 14:25 A true witness delivereth souls ...

How wonderful to have our lives be true testimonies that God can use in delivering souls from the darkness we once lived in!

CALL UPON ME AND I WILL SHOW YOU GREAT AND MIGHTY THINGS ...

After Cain was judged, he went out from the presence of the Lord. Adam and Eve then had a son they named Seth who later had a son named Enosh. At that time a wonderful thing happened:

Genesis 4:26 ... then men began to call upon the name of the Lord.

That's when things get better. When we call upon him marvelous things begin to happen as he proves his faithfulness over and over.

Psalm 99:6 Moses and Aaron among his priests, and Samuel among those who call upon his name; they called upon the Lord, and he answered them.

He will answer you, too, my friend.

Jeremiah is one of many who the Bible records as having called upon the Lord. He is quoted about forty times in the New Testament; most of these are written in Revelation.

He lived during the final days of the nation of Israel under judgment. He never lost his God-given passion though he was rejected by his own family, endured plots against his life, suffered persecution, and conflicts with other prophets. And though he did not succeed in turning his nation back to God, he never turned his back on God or his nation. Like other prophets, he was allowed to feel what God felt. In summary, his God-given assignment was difficult to say the least.

Based on **Jeremiah 9:1** He is sometimes called "the weeping prophet."

9:1 OH, that my head were waters, and my eyes a fountain of tears, that I might weep day and night for the slain daughter of my people.

He was called by God to be a prophet in 626 B.C. during the reign of King Josiah. The stunned seventeen year old then uttered a reply quickly followed by the Lord's fore-knowledge of him.

Jeremiah 1:4-7 Then the word of the Lord came upon me, saying, Before I formed thee in the womb, I knew thee; and before thou camest forth out of the womb, I sanctified thee, and I ordained thee a prophet unto the nations. Then said I, Ah, Lord God! Behold, I cannot speak; for I am a child. But the Lord said unto me, Say not I am a child; for thou shalt go to all that I shall send thee, and whatsoever I command thee thou shalt speak.

NOTE: Seventeen year old Jeremiah complained that he was only a "child." In **Psalm 105:17**, God spoke of the then seventeen year old Joseph as a "man."

God knew what he had ordained in Jeremiah before he formed him in the womb **(1:5)** and he knew what his assignment would be (just like he does yours).

11

Now, the purpose of the lengthy introduction is to bring us to God's following declaration:

33:1-3 MOREOVER, the word of the Lord came unto Jeremiah the second time, while he was yet shut up in the court of the prison, saying, Thus saith the Lord, the maker of it, the Lord who formed it, to establish it; the Lord is his name, Call upon me, and I will answer thee, and show thee great and mighty things, which thou knowest not.

A new Christian might exceedingly rejoice over the latter part in verse 3 wherein God promised to answer and to show him great and mighty things which he knows not. I have actually done that very thing without considering the miserable condition of Jeremiah's life.

Hmmm, so he was a political prisoner charged with treason for only speaking God's word. If I were him I might have prayed, "Well, first of all, since you said you would answer me and show me great and mighty things, how about releasing me from incarceration where the stench is unbearable and what little food I have is not edible. And seeing daylight again would be great. Oh, how I would enjoy a shower with soap and ointment for these rat bites. A good hot meal would be nice, too."

As we know, God's viewpoint is way above ours. He is the Alpha and the Omega (the beginning and the end). He may speak of faraway events while we are focused on what's happening in our vision now.

In **33:1** we learned that he was in the "court of the prison" which meant that he was in the Court of the Guard in King Zedekiah's royal palace. Remarkably, he continued sending God's word to the king. An unusual situation for sure. Yes, he was bound up in the prison, but the word of God was not bound.

When obeying God, you may find yourself in some unusual settings too. Jeremiah's example is a clue for us to appreciate that we can obey God regardless of temporal situations.

Those who walk with God always reach their destination. Those who deviate from his path, plan, and purpose are running a very real risk of experiencing what is stated in:

Proverbs 1:28-29 Then shall they call upon me, but I will not answer; they shall seek me early, but they shall not find me; because they hated knowledge, and did not choose the fear of the Lord.

Fifty-eight scriptures invite believers to call upon him. You will never regret calling upon him during your lifetime. Many wonderful things will happen in response to your prayers that may not have otherwise occurred.

DEBORAH and BARAK

Deborah and Barak, fourth and fifth judges of Israel, were used by God to bring victory to his people over the Canaanites.

From **Judges 3:30** we learn that under Ehud's direction, God delivered his people from their enemies, the Moabites. They then enjoyed eighty years of peace.

Judges 4: tells us that, after losing their zeal for God, they backslid repeating the four-fold cycle common to Israel: rebellion, retribution, repentance, and restoration.

Judges 4: 1-3 And the children of Israel <u>again</u> did evil in the sight of the Lord, when Ehud was dead. And the Lord sold them into the hand of Jabin, king of Canaan, who reigned in Hazor, the captain of whose host was Sisera, who dwelt in Harosheth of the Gentiles. And the children of Israel cried unto the Lord; for he (Sisera) had nine hundred chariots of iron; and twenty years he mightily oppressed the children of Israel.

This less than desirable event had been orchestrated by God. It seems that Sisera made a career out of mightily oppressing God's people. But, all the while, God was using him to fulfill his purpose in returning his people to dependence upon him.

4:4 And Deborah, a prophetess, the wife of Lapidoth, judged Israel at that time.

Deborah is a Hebrew word (#1683) meaning "bee." It's interesting that the bee is known for its orderly motion. In our study of Deborah, we will observe her orderly motion.

Lapidoth is a Hebrew word (#3941) meaning a burning flame or torch. It has been suggested that Deborah being referred to as "the wife of Lapidoth" implied that she was a burning torch and that she may not have been married at all. She would later say (**5:7**) that she was a mother in Israel.

Other Bible women were prophets: Miriam (Exodus 15:20), Huldah (2nd Kings 22:14,) and Philip's four daughters (Acts 21:8-9.) Only Deborah was a judge and a prophetess.

4:5 And she dwelt under the palm tree of Deborah, between Ramah and Bethel in Mount Ephraim; and the children of Israel came up to her for judgment.

Israel came to her seeking wise counsel and judgment; she wasn't out soliciting business or begging people to donate to her ministry as some do today.

The next verses tell us that she sent for Barak and expected that he would already know the Lord's counsel.

4:6-7 And she sent and called Barak, the son of Abinoam, out of Kedeshnaphtali, and said unto him, Hath not the Lord God of Israel commanded, saying, Go and draw toward Mount Tabor, and take with thee ten thousand men of the children of Naphtali and of the children of Zebulun? And I will draw unto thee, to the river Kishon, Sisera, the captain of Jabin's army, with his chariots and his multitude; and I will deliver him unto thine hand.

God promised, You go; I will do. God pledged to deliver Sisera, their mighty twenty-year oppressor. Challenging Sisera with his 10,000 soldiers equipped with spears, shields, and 900 iron chariots was an overwhelming thought for Barak who had only an untrained 10,000 man army without spears, shields, or chariots. It's remarkable that Barak and his army were willing to face Sisera and his 900 chariots (ancient weapons of mass destruction) knowing that many a foot-soldier had been crushed under an iron chariot wheel. They advanced not knowing what God planned to do. My friend, we, at times must do the same. The Author and the Finisher knew full-well what he planned.

4:8 And Barak said unto her, If thou wilt go with me, then will I go; but if thou not go with me, then I will not go.

This is the only Bible record of a woman being asked to go to battle. She did go, but did not join in the fighting. Barak required more than God's promise; he must have Deborah too. Perhaps her near-by presence gave courage to his army and to him.

4:9 And she said, I will surely go with thee: notwithstanding, the journey that thou takest shall not be for thine honor; for the Lord shall sell Sisera into the

<u>hand of a woman</u>. And Deborah arose, and went with Barak to Kedesh.

Barak's journey was not for his glory and neither is yours for you. He was not allowed to share the glory of the victory God had planned. However, well over a thousand years later, he was given a place of honor by having his name listed in what is known as the Faith Hall of Fame in **Hebrews 11:32**. God remembers our obedience or lack of it and there is always a sure reward for both. It seems that Deborah and Jael were worthy of the honor of being listed in Hebrews, but they weren't whereas some other women were. You'll be introduced to Jael later in this chapter.

4:10-12 And Barak called Zebulun and Naphtali to Kedesh; and he went up with ten thousand men at his feet: and Deborah went up with him. Now Heber, the Kenite, who was of the children of Hobab, the father-in-law of Moses, had severed (separated) himself from the Kenites, and pitched his tent as far as the oak of Zaanaim, which is by Kedesh. And they showed Sisera that Barak, the son of Abinoam, was gone up to Mount Tabor.

NOTE: Moses' father-in-law was Jethro. Heber, the Kenite was a descendant of Jethro.

Without knowing the rest of this episode, one might think, "What a dirty rat. He showed the enemy where to find Barak, Deborah, and the army of the Lord." However, the knowledge of their location and pursuing them there would become their death trap. Sisera trusted Heber knowing he was aligned with his king, Jabin.

You may smile when you read a few more verses in which we learn that Heber pitched his tent right where it needed to be for God to bring the victory.

4:13 And Sisera gathered together all his chariots, even nine hundred chariots of iron, and all the people who were with him, from Harosheth of the Gentiles (nations) unto the river of Kishon.

Sisera was really licking his chops at this point. He had utilized <u>ALL</u> 900 of his iron chariots as he hastened to the battle not knowing that after losing all of them and his army too, he would end up running alone as fast as his feet could carry him into a trap set by God.

(Speaking of the hidden wisdom of God ...)

1st Corinthians 2:8 Which none of the princes of this world knew; for had they known it, they would not have crucified the Lord of glory.

4:14 And Deborah said unto Barak, Up; for this is the day in which the Lord hath delivered Sisera into thine hand. Is not the Lord gone out before thee? So Barak went down from Mount Tabor, and ten thousand men after him.

After hearing from the Lord, Deborah directed Barak into battle. The past-tense "hath delivered" is used. As far as God was concerned the victory was a done deal.

And, for those who hear and believe God, it's a done deal, also. She knew the Lord had gone before. My friend, never enter into battle without seeking God and receiving his assurance that he has gone before.

Barak's obeying Deborah's direction showed that he trusted she had heard from God. From the summit of Mt. Tabor, Barak was given a wide view of the river plane below where the enemy would soon be entrapped.

4:15 And the Lord routed Sisera, and all his chariots, and all his host, with the edge of the sword before Barak, so that Sisera alighted from his chariot, and fled away on his feet.

This is where Sisera's plan unraveled. God subdued him with a cloudburst at the river of Kishon which created the mud that immobilized his chariots and water that "swept them away." This is stated in **(5:21)** though not a part of our study. He will do the same to the enemies you face! The battle is not ours; it's the Lord's. All glory and honor is his alone.

4:16 But Barak pursued after the chariots, and after the host, unto Harosheth of the nations: and all the host of Sisera fell upon the edge of the sword; and there was not a man left.

Much to their merit, Barak and his army pursued the enemy all the way to Sisera's home turf: Harosheth. They did not turn back in the day of battle like Ephraim, the largest of the northern tribes, had done. **(Psalm 78:9)**

From their wooded hiding position, Barak and his army converged like a swarm of wasp onto the rain-drenched plane. What a sight that was for Sisera and his army!

4:17-18 Howbeit Sisera fled away on his feet to the tent of Jael, the wife of Heber, the Kenite; for there was peace between Jabin, the king of Hazor, and the house of Heber, the Kenite. And Jael went out to meet Sisera, and said unto him, Turn in, my lord, turn in to me; fear not. And when he turned in unto her into the tent, she covered him with a mantle.

Sisera felt safe taking refuge in the tent of the wife of the man who had told him Barak's whereabouts. Without Jael's husband knowing, God used him to direct Sisera and his army to defeat. You know, God can use anyone at any moment to perform his good pleasure.

Poor Sisera must have been terribly disheveled and in shock after suffering such resounding defeat. Expecting to win all; he lost all.

Perhaps Jael's covering him with a mantle was done to hide his identity or as a sign of extending personal protection.

4:19-20-21 And he said unto her, Give me, I pray thee, a little water to drink; for I am thirsty. And she opened a skin of milk, and gave him drink, and covered him. Again he said unto her, Stand in the door of the tent, and it shall be, when any man doth come and inquire of thee, and say, Is there any man here? That thou shalt say, No, Then Jael, Heber's wife, took a nail of the tent, and took a hammer in her hand, and went softly unto him, and smote the nail into his temples, and fastened it into the ground; for he was fast asleep and weary. So he died.

Isaiah 9:5 For every battle of the warrior is with confused noise, and garments rolled in blood...

Truly, battles are fought with great noise and confusion, however this battle was concluded by a woman who walked softly. Jael had been equipped in advance. From setting up many tents, she had acquired the strength needed to drive the nail clean through Sisera's temples impaling him to the ground. You, too, are acquiring strengths as you journey; strengths that are preparing you for battles ahead. Jael apparently had no advance warning of what that faithful day would hold. And neither do we know the victories God has planned for his glory.

4:22 And, behold, as Barak pursued Sisera, Jael came out to meet him, and said unto him, Come, and I will show thee the man whom thou seekest. And when he came into her tent, behold, Sisera lay dead, and the nail was in his temples.

I like this man Barak. He entered Jael's tent not knowing he would find his enemy dead; killed by one woman and one nail. Just as he had been told by Deborah (4:9) the enemy was defeated by the hand of a woman.

4:23-24 So God subdued on that day Jabin the king of Canaan before the children of Israel. And the hand of the children of Israel prospered and prevailed against Jabin the king of Canaan until they had destroyed Jabin, king of Canaan.

Judges 5:31 states that following the victory won through Deborah and Barak, the people enjoyed forty years of peace.

The selfless courageous acts of Deborah and Barak together with ten thousand footmen provided a forty year span of peace. During this drama, they had no way of knowing what God had determined. They only saw an insurmountable obstacle; God saw the reward of their obedience.

Likewise, your love and devotion to God shown by your obedience to him will result in manifold blessings to you and others as God's kaleidoscope causes every detail to fall into place.

HOW LONG?

During the space shuttle Discovery's final voyage in March 2011, U. S. Astronaut-Space-Walker Stephen Bowen was precariously perched on a small platform at the end of the 58-foot robotic-arm 220 miles above the Earth when he asked Mission Control, "How long?" He was told that the trouble, caused by a robotic system shutdown, would be resolved soon. The following thirty-minutes must have seemed like thirty years, as he waited for fellow astronauts inside the spacecraft to successfully activate the robotic-arm.

You may never be suspended in outer space and asking, "How long?" But chances are that question will arise many times during your earthly voyage.

And that may be partially because, unlike other animals, our Creator made man to be aware of the passing of time. Therefore, waiting can be especially difficult.

We are not alone, however, in asking the "How long?" question. Scripture records it being asked at least thirty-seven times. Psalmists asked this question fifteen times and Jesus himself asked it twice.

Following his mountaintop exhilarating transfiguration, Jesus encountered an epileptic boy that his disciples hadn't been able to heal. Expressing his disappointment and frustration, he scolded:

Matthew 17:17 O faithless and perverse generation, how long shall I be with you? How long shall I bear with you?

Fifteen psalms written by King David, the sons of Korah, and Moses all ask the question, "How long?"

Can you guess who the Bible reveals asking the "How long?" question more than any other? The answer may surprise you. It is God himself! The Author of time asked "How long?" at least eight times.

The first "how long" question was recorded in **Exodus 10:3** when God asked Pharaoh, "Thus saith the Lord God of the Hebrews, How long wilt thou refuse to humble thyself before me?

Exodus 16:28 How long refuse ye to keep my commandments?

Numbers 14:11 How long will this people provoke me? And how long will it be before they believe me, for all the signs which I have shown among them?

Number 14:27 How long shall I bear with this evil congregation, who murmur against me?

1st Samuel 16:1 How long wilt thou mourn for Saul, seeing I have rejected him from reigning over Israel?

Jeremiah 23:26 How long shall this be in the hearts of the prophets that prophesy lies?

Jeremiah 31:22 How long wilt thou go about, O thou backsliding daughter?

We know, of course, that the only limitations God has are self-imposed. Within that thought lies the answer to

24

"How long?"

When he is satisfied and his purposes served, like the Israelites, you will hear him say:

Deuteronomy 1:6 The Lord God spoke unto us in Herob, saying, Ye, have dwelt <u>long enough</u> in this mount; turn you, and take your journey ...

JOSEPH THE PATRIARCH
Genesis 37:2 – 50:21

Our study of the life of the patriarch Joseph begins with Genesis 37:2 where we are told he is seventeen years old. He and his family had been in Canaan's land eleven years. His grandparents, Isaac and Rebekah, had died. And his mother, Rachel, had also died following the birth of Joseph's brother Benjamin.

37:2 states that Joseph was with the sons of Bilhah (Dan and Naphtali,) and the sons of Zilpah (Gad and Asher) and that he reported their evil to his father. We are not told what evil or bad deed his half-brothers had done. It may have been that his father had required him to report any misdeeds of his older half-brothers who were born of concubines: Bilah and Zilpah. Joseph did not participate in their evil, and neither did he cover it up. His reporting of their misdeed to their mutual father didn't foster a bond of brotherly love. The word "evil" used here is the Hebrew word (#7451) meaning "exceedingly great harm" which confirmed the seriousness of their misconduct.

Following Joseph's reporting of his half-brothers' evil, his father presented him with the special coat of many colors; which could actually be called "a coat of many troubles." It might have been that the special coat was given to honor Joseph's integrity which he was to exhibit throughout his lifetime.

37:3-4 Now Israel (Jacob) loved Joseph more than all his children, because he was the son of his old age: and made him a coat of many colors. And when his brethren saw that their father loved him more than all his brethren, they hated him, and could not speak peaceably unto him.

The words "loved" and "hate" are used in the same scripture. Jacob loved and his sons hated. We will find later that his brothers hated not only Joseph, but their father too. Imagine how intense their relationship had become that they could not even speak peaceably to Joseph. It's a wonder that Jacob showed such outward favoritism after having experienced severe, distressing sibling rivalry created by his mother favoring him over his brother Esau. Such favoritism goes a long way to create a hostile hurtful family environment.

The coat of many colors was a long-sleeved, full-length tunic designed to be a special honor and a mark of distinction. Ordinarily such a garment would have been given to the firstborn son as an indication that the father intended him to become the head of the family. However, Reuben, Jacob's firstborn son, had already forfeited this privilege by defiling his father's concubine Bilhah **(Genesis 35:22)**. Jacob would later say Reuben was "unstable as water."

37:5-7 And Joseph dreamed a dream, and he told it to his brethren: and they hated him yet the more. And he said unto them, Hear, I pray you, this dream which I have dreamed. For, behold, we were binding sheaves in the field, and, lo, my sheaf arose, and also stood upright; and, behold, your sheaves stood round about, and made obeisance to my sheaf.

This young seventeen year old lad lacked the wisdom to know when to speak and when not to speak. As we all know, a good portion of the wisdom we acquire comes by experience. However, when we are mature enough to know that we lack the wisdom to be victorious over our adversities, we learn to do as James instructed.

James 1:5 If any of you lack wisdom, let him ask God, who giveth to all men liberally, and upbraideth not, and it shall be given unto him.

We'll learn, as Joseph's life continued, he did gain the wisdom to know when to speak and when not to speak. I will be glad when that wisdom is imparted to me!

Joseph made the unfortunate, naive choice of using the word "obeisance," which is a Hebrew word (#7812) meaning "to humbly beseech, to show reverence, to worship." Such a choice of words leads the reader to believe that Joseph was oblivious to the hate already directed toward him.

37:8-9 And his brethren said to him, Shalt thou indeed reign over us? Or shalt thou indeed have dominion over us? And they hated him yet the more for his dreams, and for his words. And he dreamed yet another dream, and told it to his brethren, and said, Behold, I have dreamed a dream more; and behold, the sun and the moon and the eleven stars made obeisance to me.

Wow! Joseph was told by dreams that not only would his eleven brothers show him obeisance but also two higher authorities would do the same. He would later draw strength and courage when remembering those dreams. In the providence of God, Joseph's telling of the dreams actually facilitated God's purposes, as we will come to understand.

37:10-11 And he told it to his father, and to his brethren; and his father rebuked him, What is this dream that thou hast dreamed? Shall I and thy mother and thy brethren indeed come to bow down ourselves to thee to the earth? And his brethren envied him; but his father observed the saying.

Jacob, knowing that an angel of God had spoken to him in a dream **(31:10-13)**, was more cautious to observe and not to condemn Joseph having such dreams. However, the seeds of hatred had already been sown deep within his other sons' hearts. Joseph naïvely sharing his dreams caused these deeply rooted seeds to sprout and produce actions.

Proverbs 27:4 plainly states: Wrath is cruel, and anger is outrageous, but who is able to stand before envy?

Two scriptures state that Pilate "knew that for envy they had delivered him (Jesus)". **Matthew 27:18, Mark 15:10**

Here is a progression of thoughts:

Mark 7:21-23 For from within, out of the heart of men, proceed evil thoughts, adulteries, fornications, murders, thefts, covetousness, wickedness, deceit, lasciviousness (evil desire,) an evil eye, blasphemy, pride, foolishness. All these evil things come from within, and defile the man.

Now back to our study of Joseph:

37:12-14 And his brethren went to feed their father's flock in Shechem. And Israel (Jacob) said unto Joseph, Do not thy brethren feed the flock in Shechem? Come, and I will send thee unto them. And he said unto him, Here I am. And he said unto him, Go, I pray thee, see whether it be well with thy brethren, and well with the flocks; and bring me word again. So he sent him out of the vale (valley) of Hebron, and he came to Shechem.

We can only wonder why Joseph was not with his brothers attending the flocks. Perhaps this was another sign of his father's favoritism.

The ancient city of Shechem has great significance. It is located some thirty miles south of Jerusalem and is where Jacob's well is still producing water. This is where Jesus met the woman at the well recorded in **John 4.** Shechem had been designated as a city of refuge. Joseph's tomb was vandalized there by Arabs in October 2000.

37:15-17 And a certain man found him, and, behold he was wandering in the field: and the man asked him, saying, What seekest thou? And he said, I seek my brethren: tell me, I pray thee, where they feed their flocks. And the man said, They are departed from here; for I heard them say, Let us go to Dothan. And Joseph went after his brethren, and found them in Dothan.

Who was this providentially placed unnamed man who was able to point Joseph in the right direction? The scripture said that Joseph was wandering. He didn't know which way to go. We can always count on God to make a way for his assignments to be accomplished.

Dothan, some fifteen miles north of Shechem, was a strategic trade location forming a crossroads for merchants and traders traveling to Egypt. That was where they all needed to be in order for God to advance his plan and purpose.

37:18-19 And when they saw him afar off, even before he came near unto them, they conspired against him to slay him. And they said one to another, Behold, this dreamer cometh.

This is the only time the Bible uses this Hebrew word (#5230) "conspire" which means "to act treacherously or to betray a trust." This is what envy and jealously will bring a person to.

Their evil thoughts continued in:

verse 20 Come now therefore, and let us slay him, and cast him into some pit, and we will say, Some evil beast hath devoured him: and we shall see what will become of his dreams.

They would all live to see what would become of Joseph's God-given dreams as God worked wondrously to perform his will.

Reuben stated his objection to their murderous plot:

37:21-22 And Reuben heard it, and he delivered him out of their hands; and said, Let us not kill him. And Reuben said unto them, Shed no blood, but cast him into this pit that is in the wilderness, and lay no hand upon him; that he might rid him out of their hands, to deliver him to his father again.

Some say, "Let us slay him," while Reuben implored, "Let us not kill him." Scripture uses the phrase, "Let us," fifteen times with some being invitations to do evil and others being admonishments to do good. This can be called (smile) the "lettuce syndrome," where a mob mentality reigns or a more reasonable conclusion is reached by group counsel.

Reuben's thought of delivering Joseph from his brothers and returning him to their father had much merit. Throughout this study we will find that only Reuben and Joseph actually had heartfelt concern for their father. The younger brother, Benjamin, had been left at home and was not a part of this scheme.

37:23-24 And it came to pass, when Joseph was come unto his brethren, that they stripped Joseph out of his coat of many colors that was on him; and they took him, and cast him into a pit: and the pit was empty, and there was no water in it.

They stripped him of the coveted garment that had set him apart from the others. We are not told of Joseph's reaction to facing his brothers' murderess mob mentality. He was beginning to experience his God-given dreams becoming a nightmare. As the reality of his new circumstance sets in, let's read the actions of his ten self-serving brothers.

37:25 And they sat down to eat bread: and they lifted up their eyes and looked, and behold, a company of Ishmaelites came from Gilead with their camels bearing spicery and balm and myrrh, going to carry it down to Egypt.

With no regard for their younger brother, they sat down to eat. How charming. They sat down to eat while their dejected brother was left alone in a sweltering, deep, waterless pit. No doubt though, as they ate, their hatred for him was eating them too.

Then Judah was struck with an idea by which they can not only rid themselves of Joseph but can also put a little jingle in their pockets. His neat and nifty plan easily persuaded the brothers.

37:26-27 And Judah said unto his brethren, What profit is it if we slay our brother, and conceal his blood? Come, and let us sell him to the Ishmaelites, and let not our hand be upon him, for he is our brother and our flesh. And his brethren were content.

What an inspiring humanitarian thought! This is where the "lettuce syndrome" kicked in again. They acknowledged that he is their brother, and he is their blood. Is this the beginning of their having an actual conscience? No, not at all. The thought that they won't have to kill him or even have his blood upon their hands and, yet, they can profit from his disposal is too tantalizing to ignore.

Let us remember that these ten brothers didn't have the written law of God as their guide or indwelling Emanuel as we do. But they did have what is called the "Adamic nature" or the "fallen nature" of unregenerated man.

37:28 Then there passed by Midianites, merchantmen; and they drew and lifted up Joseph out of the pit, and sold Joseph to the Ishmaelites for twenty pieces of silver: and they brought Joseph into Egypt.

What emotional condition was Joseph in? Did they respond to his desperate pleas for help? How long was Joseph in the desert pit? While being lifted up by his brothers, was he thinking that they were rescuing him? It will be decades in his life's saga before we are given insight into his emotions.

The Midianites and Ishmaelites are thought to be the same group who were descendants of Abraham's son Ishmael. They were coming west from Gilead and were headed to Egypt intending to sell their spices, balm, and myrrh. Purchasing Joseph meant they would have a little extra to sell when they arrived in Egypt.

How did Joseph feel by his entire life's course changing drastically within such a short time? We know that his life's circumstance had to change in order for God to perform the things he had appointed unto him.

You are encouraged by this writing to allow God to change your life's direction and or circumstance even suddenly for his glory. He is the Alpha and the Omega. He knows the beginning and the end of you, dear one.

No one has ever been known to bow down to a slave. His new-reality mocked his God-given expectations which had now begun to be to be severely tested. It is thought that he was sold into slavery in approximately 1897 B.C.

37:29-30 And Reuben returned unto the pit, and behold, Joseph was not in the pit; and he rent (tore) his clothes. And he returned unto his brethren, and said, The child is not; and I, where shall I go?

Apparently, Reuben had been out of the area while the sale of Joseph was taking place. Reuben knew the pit was too deep for Joseph to escape on his own. His reaction upon his return demonstrated his deep concern. I wonder if he was a partaker on their bounty.

37:31-32 And they took Joseph's coat, and killed a kid of the goats, and dipped the coat in blood; and they sent the coat of many colors, and they brought it to their father; and said, This have we found: know now whether it be thy son's coat or not.

37:33-35 And he knew it, and said, It is my son's coat; an evil beast hath devoured him; Joseph is without doubt torn to pieces. And Jacob rent (tore) his clothes, and put sackcloth upon his loins, and mourned for his son many days. And all his sons and all his daughters rose up to comfort him; but he refused to be comforted; and he said, For I will go down into the grave (Sheol) unto my son mourning. Thus his father wept for him.

The brothers' emotions are not recorded. We are left to wonder how they felt while seeing the inconsolable anguish of their father over a long period of time. Were they so callous as to not be affected by what so deeply affected Jacob? Did they hate Jacob as they had hated Joseph? Why did they drench Joseph's coat in goat's blood? The coat – always the coat – the very object that set Joseph apart from them and elevated him to a superior position of respect and authority. How they must have hated that coat, too. Why did they not simply tell their father that Joseph fell, hit his head on a rock, died, and that they buried him?

Upon seeing the bloody coat of many colors, he assumed Joseph had been torn to pieces and devoured by a wild beast. This thought was exceptionally grievous to Jacob since there would be no corpse to bury. And, without a body, how could he be certain that Joseph was dead and not just injured? To be eaten by wild beasts and to be left without a body to bury was tantamount to total disgrace that left the mourners with unending grief. The brothers daily observed their father's torment. God required the dead to be buried. A body unburied would defile the land. (**Deuteronomy 21:23** and **Ezekiel 39:14**.)

37:36 And the Midianites sold him into Egypt unto Potiphar, an officer of Pharaoh's, and captain of the guard.

We cannot envision the thoughts of seventeen-year-old Joseph as his new reality contradicts his God-given expectations. By the way, though not as severe, you will experience contradictions as you journey to the glory world also.

NOTE: "Pharaoh" is a general term used to refer to all Egyptian kings.

Genesis
Chapter 39

The Bible account of the life of Joseph contains the statement, "and it came to pass," nineteen times. Eight of those times are recorded in Chapter 39 where we learn of some amazing events in young Joseph's life as well as some horrific ones. It's as though the writer wanted us to know that what "came to pass" didn't come to stay. At this point, Joseph had gone from being the favored son of his father to being a slave in a foreign land; he had gone from the pit to the palace.

39:1 And Joseph was brought down to Egypt; and Potiphar, an officer of Pharaoh, captain of the guard, an Egyptian, bought him of the hands of the Ishmaelites, who had brought him down there.

Joseph was <u>brought</u> and then he was <u>bought</u>. All of this must have seemed surreal to Joseph. His life is wildly out of his control. He is now a slave in a foreign country among people whose language and customs he did not understand. He is totally alone and without the written word of God. This young man felt deep hurt, confusion, and betrayal. Few people experience such sudden and devastating changes in their lives as did Joseph. Scripture does not expose his emotions until much later after many years of his life's saga had passed.

39:2-4 And the Lord was with Joseph, and he was a prosperous man; and he was in the house of his master, the Egyptian. And his master saw that the Lord was with him, and that the Lord made all that he did to prosper in his hand. And Joseph found grace in his sight, and he served him: and he made him overseer over his house, and all that he had he put into his hand.

We are given five scriptures that state, "the Lord was with Joseph." Four are found in this chapter and another in **Acts 7:9** where Stephen, the first martyr, addressed the Sanhedrin and declared, "And the patriarchs, moved with envy, sold Joseph into Egypt; but God was with him."

Enduring what seemed like unending hardships while doing your best and yet being falsely accused and condemned are never pleasant sought-after experiences; however to know that God is with you anchors your soul.

Joseph's adjustment to his new circumstance seems obvious. He knew that God was with him. Did he wonder why he wasn't delivered from his captivity? Did he question God as to why all of this injustice had come upon him as we sometimes do?

As previously noted, Egyptians worshiped numerous "little g" gods". It is noteworthy that Potiphar also knew that God (the one true God of the Hebrews) was with Joseph. Potiphar placed in him tremendous favor and trust.

39:5-6 And it came to pass from the time that he had made him overseer in his house, and over all that he had, that the Lord blessed the Egyptian's house for Joseph's sake; and the blessing of the Lord was upon all that he had in the house, and in the field. And he left all that he had in Joseph's hand; and he knew not anything he had, save the food which he did eat. And Joseph was a handsome person, and well favored.

By Joseph's having godly behavior, he had won the complete trust of Potiphar. He never deviated from what he had been taught by his Hebrew upbringing. It's interesting that we are only now told that Joseph was a handsome young man. His being handsome, though, is going to create another great dilemma for him.

39:7-9 And it came to pass after these things, that his master's wife cast her eyes upon Joseph; and she said, Lie with me. But he refused, and said unto his master's wife, Behold my master knoweth not what is with me in the house, and he hath committed all that he hath in my hand; there is none greater in this house than I; neither hath he kept back anything from me but thee, because thou art his wife. How then can I do this great wickedness, and sin against God?

What a heart for God was in young Joseph! Why should this young lad be concerned about the possibility of sinning against God? It looks like God had dealt him a few undeserved blows from which he had no hope of escaping. Why not enjoy the pleasures of sin? And yet Joseph discerned her proposition as "great wickedness." Joseph not only refused her flirtation out of respect for God but also for Potiphar.

Joseph respected Potiphar when even his wife didn't. Most men would need a hazmat suit to avoid her contamination as she stealthily stalked her prey. However, all Joseph needed, he already had; the abiding presence of the God of the Hebrews.

39:10-12 And it came to pass, as she spoke to Joseph day by day, that he hearkened not unto her, to lie with her, or to be with her. And it came to pass about this time, that Joseph went into the house to do his work; and there was none of the men of the house there within. And she caught him by his garment, saying, Lie with me: and he left his garment in her hand, and fled, and got out.

This woman went after him relentlessly day by day. This wasn't a one-time attempt to entice him. She had cast her eye upon him, and she was determined to have her way.

Joseph, knowing the never-named wife of Potiphar had cast her eye upon him, innocently entered the house when no other household servant was there. The calculating wife seized the opportunity to feed her lust.

Well, this is the second garment young terror-stricken Joseph had left behind. He fled the house as soon as he could. This was a dramatic debacle with no happy ending in sight. My heart quakes for Joseph.

39:13-15 And it came to pass, when she saw that he had left his garment in her hand, and was fled forth, that she called the men of her house, and spoke unto them saying, See, he hath brought in a Hebrew unto us to mock us; he came in unto me to lie with me, and I cried with a loud voice. And it came to pass, when he heard that I lifted up my voice and cried, that he left his garment with me, and fled, and got out.

She carefully diverted blame to her husband when she told the men servants, "He (Potiphar) hath brought in a Hebrew unto us to mock us." She'll use this blame-shifting technique again when she attempted to put responsibility unto Potiphar again. Sometimes I am tempted to think of this man as "Potiphar, the pitifully pathetic man." But that would be unkind since he too had been catapulted into a challenging unforeseen circumstance. Loyalty to his wife and admiration for his servant may have put him in conflict with his conscience.

39:16-20 And she laid up his garment by her, until his lord came home. And she spoke unto him according to these words, saying, The Hebrew servant, <u>whom thou hast brought unto us</u>, came unto me to mock me. And it came to pass, as I lifted up my voice and cried, that he left his garment with me, and fled. And it came to pass, when his master heard the words of his wife, which she spoke unto him saying, After this manner did <u>thy servant</u> to me, that his wrath was kindled. And Joseph's master took him, and put him into the prison, a place where the king's prisoners were bound: and he was there in the prison.

So Joseph journeyed from the pit to the palace and from the palace to the prison without understanding why. His experience didn't line up with what his God-given dreams foretold. The young Joseph had every right

42

to be dismayed and to turn his heart away from God, **but** he didn't. He didn't ask like Gideon in **Judges 6:13**, "O my Lord, if the Lord be with us, why then is all this befallen us?

Potiphar's contemptable wife skillfully placed the blame for her suffering such a horrific ordeal at the hands of the Hebrew servant, <u>whom thou hast brought unto us</u> upon her husband. She further pointed out that this Hebrew is <u>thy servant</u>.

It's curious that Potiphar didn't have him immediately executed as would be the custom, but, instead, had him committed to the prison located directly below his house. This sort of makes you wonder if Potiphar entirely believed his wife's accusation.

We are not told that Joseph was given a chance to defend himself or that he ever made a denunciation of the repugnant accusation. He was unjustly accused, condemned, and sent to a prison where only the king's prisoners were held.

We are not told that the unnamed wife of Potiphar ever expressed remorse for causing an innocent foreign young man to be imprisoned. Of course, that's not a surprise.

We have read scriptures stating that Potiphar knew God was with Joseph. We are left to wonder what Potiphar thought of Joseph and his God after the accusations of his wife.

39:21 But the Lord was with Joseph, and showed him mercy, and gave him, favor in the sight of the keeper of the prison.

Well, here we go again. God is with Joseph. He caused him to have favor with the keeper of the prison. And, yet, God doesn't deliver him from this misfortune.

39:22-23 And the keeper of the prison committed to Joseph's hand all the prisoners that were in the prison; and whatsoever they did there, he was the doer of it. The keeper of the prison looked not to anything that was under his hand; because the Lord was with him, and that which he did, the Lord made to prosper.

True enough, God blessed all that Joseph did but the fact remains that he was still a youth who was a slave-prisoner in a foreign land, who was hated by his brothers, and who was deeply mourned by his father. At best, his life's circumstance was less than deserved or desired.

Genesis
Chapter 40

40:1-4 And it came to pass after these things, that the butler of the king of Egypt, and his baker, had offended their lord, the king of Egypt. And Pharaoh was angry with two of his officers, against the chief of the butlers, and against the chief of the bakers. And he put them in prison in the house of the captain of the guard, into the prison, the place where Joseph was bound. And the captain of the guard charged Joseph with them, and he served them: and they continued a season in prison.

Being in the king's service was a risky position. The king literally held their lives in his hands. We are not told what their offenses were. Perhaps these offenses existed only in the mind of Pharaoh. These men were taken from their workplaces without any regard for their families or lives. The length of their stay would be determined by the whim of the king.

The highly favored Joseph was in charge of the other prisoners and he "served" them for a "season." Only God knows the length of the seasons he has determined. The length of the season may depend largely on the accomplishment of his will.

40:5-7 And they dreamed a dream both of them, each man his dream in one night, each man according to the interpretation of his dream, the butler and the baker of the king of Egypt, who were bound in the prison. And Joseph came in unto them in the morning, and looked upon them, and, behold, they were sad. And he asked

Pharaoh's officers who were with him in the prison of his lord's house, saying, Wherefore look ye so sad today?

Joseph had a merciful and tender heart which caused him to take note of the sadness of the other prisoners and to inquire, "Wherefore look ye so sad?" Why wouldn't they be continually sad? After all, they were in prison for an undetermined amount of time. At best, their futures were uncertain. That would be cause enough for a great deal of sadness.

40:8-11 And they said unto him, We have dreamed a dream, and there is no interpreter of it. And Joseph said unto them, Do not interpretations belong to God? Tell me them, I pray you. And the chief butler told his dream to Joseph, and said to him, In my dream, behold, a vine was before me; And in the vine were three branches: and it was as though it budded, and her blossoms shot forth; and the clusters thereof brought forth ripe grapes. And Pharaoh's cup was in my hand: and I took the grapes, and pressed them into Pharaoh's cup, and I gave the cup into Pharaoh's hand.

Oneiromancy, the ancient art of dream interpretation, flourished in Egypt because dreams were thought to foretell the future. Naturally, everyone wants to know the future. The butler and baker were distressed thinking that their dreams foretold their futures but they didn't have anyone to explain their meanings.

Joseph could have said that he had had a couple of wild dreams himself but that they proved to be false. But, no, he confidently directed them to God, and

46

declared, "Do not interpretations belong to God?" His steadfast faith in the God of the Hebrews was truly amazing.

40:12-15 And Joseph said unto him, This is the interpretation of it: The three branches are three days. Yet within three days shall Pharaoh lift up thine head, and restore thee into thy place: and thou shalt deliver Pharaoh's cup into his hand, after the former manner when thou wast his butler. But think on me when it shall be well with thee, and show kindness, I pray thee, unto me, and make mention of me unto Pharaoh, and bring me out of this house. For indeed I was stolen away out of the land of the Hebrews: and here also have I done nothing that they should put me into this dungeon.

This is the only recorded instance where Joseph asked anyone for anything. He asked to be remembered and that kindness be shown him. He doesn't proclaim his worthiness. He doesn't say that his brothers hated him and wickedly sold him into slavery. He merely said, "For I was stolen away out of the land of the Hebrews." He referred to the land of Canaan as "the land of the Hebrews" knowing full well that God had promised the land to them in the covenant he made with Abraham.

40:16-19 When the chief baker saw that the interpretation was good, he said unto Joseph, I also was in my dream, and, behold, I had three white baskets on my head. And in the uppermost basket there were all manner of foods for Pharaoh; and the birds did eat them out of the basket upon my head. And Joseph answered and said, This is the interpretation thereof: The three baskets are three days. Yet within three days shall Pharaoh <u>lift up thy head from off thee</u>, and shall hang thee on a tree; and the birds shall eat thy flesh from off thee.

The chief baker had been anxious to hear Joseph's dream interpretation since the butler had received such an reassuring one. In Joseph's interpretation to the butler, he said his head would be lifted up, but to the baker, he said his head would be lifted off.

40:20-23 And it came to pass the third day, which was Pharaoh's birthday, that he made a feast unto all his servants; and he lifted up the head of the chief butler and of the chief baker among his servants. And he restored the chief butler unto his butlership again; and he gave the cup into Pharaoh's hand. But he hanged the chief baker: as Joseph had interpreted to them. Yet did not the chief butler remember Joseph, but forgot him.

Can you see Joseph languishing in prison while his youth ebbs away as he waits and wonders whatever became of the butler or of his request to be remembered? Did he question why the dreams of the butler and the baker were fulfilled according to his interpretation yet his God-given dreams were contradicted and unfulfilled? This was not a fairy tale; it happened as written. All the events and people were real.

48

How about the unfortunate baker who lost his head by the whim of Pharaoh? Just the thought would make anyone grimace.

Genesis
Chapter 41

41:1 And it came to pass at the end of two full years, that Pharaoh dreamed: and, behold, he stood by the river.

Here we go with yet another dream. Joseph dreamed, the butler dreamed, the baker dreamed, and now the Pharaoh himself had a dream. The scripture said, "two full years," and not, "two short years." During this time, Joseph existed in a miserable, undeserved predicament.

41:2-8 And, behold, there came up out of the river seven well favored cows and fat fleshed; and they fed in the meadow. And, behold, seven other cows came up after them out of the river, ill-favored and lean fleshed; and stood by the other cows upon the brink of the river. And the ill-favored and lean fleshed cows did eat up the seven well favored and fat cows. So Pharaoh awoke. And he slept and dreamed the second time: and, behold, seven ears of grain came up upon one stalk, full and good. And, behold, seven thin ears and blighted with the east wind sprung up after them. And the seven thin ears devoured the seven fat and full ears. And Pharaoh awoke, and, behold, it was a dream. And it came to pass in the morning that his spirit was troubled; and he sent and called for all the magicians of Egypt, and all the wise men thereof: and Pharaoh told them his dream; but there was none that could interpret them unto Pharaoh.

As noted earlier, Egyptians knew that dreams could have great significance. Pharaoh was disturbed by his dreams and was determined to learn their meaning.

Pharaoh summonsed ALL of the Egyptian magicians. That must have been a huge gathering!

The memory of dreaming of the fat and lean was vivid. Pharaoh knew he had to know the interpretation.

Even today, with well cultivated and fertilized fields, one corn stalk generally only yields three ears. What did his dream mean when he saw stalks yielding seven ears? And, what did his dream mean when he saw the blighted lean corn? By the providence of God, no interpreter was found.

41:9-13 Then spoke the chief butler unto Pharaoh, saying, I do remember my faults this day. Pharaoh was angry with his servants, and put me in prison in the captain of the guard's house, both me and the chief baker. And we dreamed a dream in one night, I and he; we dreamed each man according to the interpretation of his dream. And there was there with us a <u>young</u> man, a Hebrew, servant to the captain of the guard; and we told him, and he interpreted to us our dreams; to each man according to the interpretation of his dream. And it came to pass, as he interpreted to us, so it was; me he restored unto mine office, and him he hanged.

The chief butler had been at liberty two full years before he remembered his fault in not helping Joseph. Well, it was about time he remembered. But, of course, we know it was all accomplished in God's timing.

Without giving Joseph's name, which perhaps he couldn't recall, he described him as a "young Hebrew." Even after all that Joseph had been through, he was still a youth. The strength of this young Hebrew's virtue has inspired others (including me) for thousands of years.

41:14-16 Then Pharaoh sent and called Joseph, and they brought him hastily out of the dungeon: and he shaved himself, and changed his raiment, and came in unto Pharaoh. And Pharaoh said unto Joseph, I have dreamed a dream, and there is none that can interpret it: and I have heard say of thee, that thou canst understand a dream to interpret it. And Joseph answered Pharaoh, saying, It is not in me; God shall give Pharaoh an answer of peace.

Proverbs 18:16 A man's gift maketh room for him, and bringeth him before great men.

God had equipped Joseph with the gift of interpreting dreams. This gift did make room for him, and it brought him before the king. (Chances are that yours will too.)

Being housed in the prison dungeon meant that Joseph's appearance wasn't exactly presentable. He hastily readied himself by shaving and changing into fresh clothes.

And, as amazing as that is, Joseph's answer is even more amazing. "It is not in me; God will give Pharaoh an answer of peace." The confidence that Joseph maintained in his God is nothing short of astonishing.

Pharaoh had absolute rule over the entire Egyptian empire, but he didn't have the peace that Joseph promised his God would give him. Surely Joseph was experiencing God's peace himself.

It is too marvelous for words to express that regardless of the temporal circumstance, we are promised in: **Philippians 4:7** And the peace of God that passeth all understanding, shall keep your hearts and minds through Christ Jesus.

How could Joseph speak so assuredly to a man who could order his immediate death as he had done to others? Note that Joseph promised his God would give him peace even before he had heard Pharaoh's two dreams. Amazing.

41:17-24 And Pharaoh said unto Joseph, In my dream, behold, I stood upon the bank of the river. And, behold, there came up out of the river seven cows, fat fleshed and well favored; and they fed in a meadow. And, behold, seven other cows came up after them, poor and very ill favored and lean fleshed, such as I never saw in all the land of Egypt for badness. And the lean and the ill-favored cows did eat up the first seven fat cows. And when they had eaten them up, it could not be known that they had eaten them; but they were still ill favored, as at the beginning. So I awoke. And I saw in my dream, and, behold, seven ears came up in one stalk, full and good. And, behold, seven ears, withered, thin, and blighted with the east wind, sprung up after them. And the thin ears devoured the seven good ears; and I told this unto the magicians; but there was none that could declare it to me.

Perhaps the thought of a destructive east wind was as alarming to Pharaoh as seeing the good ears of corn being devoured by the lean ears. The term "east wind" is used nineteen times in scripture. God sent the east wind to bring judgment and to accomplish his purposes. He used the east wind to dry up the Red Sea some 430 years later. Also, at that time, he used the east wind to bring swarms of locusts. He sent a vehement east wind in an attempt to get Jonah's attention. And, **Acts 27:14** records that Paul and Luke, while sailing to Rome, were caught in a Euroclydon (east) wind.

For additional East Wind information see the story of Jonah later in this book.

41:25 And Joseph said unto Pharaoh, The dream of Pharaoh is one: God hath shown Pharaoh what he is about to do.

What unwavering confidence in God! Joseph placed his own life on the line by declaring what his God was going to do. Joseph then began his interpretation.

41:26-28 The seven good cows are seven years; and the seven good ears are seven years: the dream is one. And the seven thin and ill-favored cows that came up after them are seven years; and the seven empty ears blighted with the east wind shall be seven years of famine. This is the thing which I have spoken unto

Pharaoh: What God is about to do he showeth unto Pharaoh.

Joseph again spoke to Pharaoh about his God. This, in itself, is remarkable considering that the Egyptians worshiped many so-called gods. Pharaoh could not have expressed confidence in any of his false gods. But Joseph's God was going to demonstrate to him exactly who he was. Without bringing recognition to himself by saying, "God has shown me what he's going to do," he declared that God was showing his plans to Pharaoh.

41:29-32 Behold, there come seven years of great plenty throughout all the land of Egypt. And there shall arise after them seven years of famine; and all the plenty shall be forgotten in the land of Egypt; and the famine shall consume the land; And the plenty shall not be known in the land by reason of that famine following; for it shall be very grievous. And for that the dream was doubled unto Pharaoh twice; it is because the thing is established by God, and God will shortly bring it to pass.

Joseph did not indicate that God may have had reasons for warning Pharaoh in advance or had reasons for allowing the famine at all. The dreams did get Pharaoh's full attention though and caused him to completely believe Joseph's interpretation. The severity of the seven year famine is stressed by Joseph, and its impact was chiseled onto Pharaoh's conscience by the vivid twice-repeated dream. Pharaoh and his counselors did not need to be reminded of the devastation caused by previous famines. They knew that famine meant starvation of all living things, plus a crushing blow to their kingdom.

41:33-37 Now therefore let Pharaoh seek out a man discreet and wise, and set him over the land of Egypt. Let Pharaoh do this, and let him appoint officers over the land, and take up the fifth part of the land of Egypt in the seven plenteous years. And let them gather all the food of those good years that come, and lay up grain under the hand of Pharaoh, and let them keep food in the cities. And that food shall be for storage in the land against the seven years of famine, which shall be in the land of Egypt; that the land perish not through the famine. And the thing was good in the eyes of Pharaoh, and in the eyes of all his servants.

Joseph, a slave, prisoner, and foreigner, was not thinking of himself as he described the type of man needed to secure Egypt's survival during the seven year famine. Pharaoh knew the seriousness of choosing the right man.

41:38 And Pharaoh said unto his servants, Can we find such a one as this is, a man in whom the Spirit of God is?

Throughout this entire discourse, Joseph had centered his response on God and had mentioned his name six times. He used the Hebrew word (#4130) "Eloheem" which means "God of Israel." But, here in verse :38, Pharaoh himself used the same word in recognizing that the God of Israel is the Spirit God who was in Joseph. Amazing, totally amazing.

Pharaoh and his servants are in awe of Joseph as they acknowledged that he was the one man for the difficult and necessary tasks ahead.

41:39-41 And Pharaoh said unto Joseph, Forasmuch as God hath shown thee all this, there is none as discreet and wise as thou art. Thou shalt be over my house, and according unto thy word shall all my people be ruled: only in the throne will I be greater than thou. And Pharaoh said unto Joseph, See, I have set thee over all the land of Egypt.

Here again Pharaoh acknowledged that the God of the Hebrews was true. He exalted Joseph to a position of great authority, which was quite a distance from the dungeon where he had woken up that morning. He was given Pharaoh's Blue Ribbon of Approval and was given Cart Blanche over all of Egypt.

Our hero, Joseph, had gone from his father's pasture, to the pit, to the palace, from the palace to the prison, and now, from the prison to the palace again.

And with this sudden change in status came great authority. Pharaoh said that by him would "all my people be ruled." Well, I guess that would include Potiphar and his lust-filled wife. It is nowhere written that Joseph used his delegated authority to retaliate against Potiphar or his wife. Doing something like that wouldn't be characteristic of the Joseph written about in

God's word. He remained steadfast as he gave honor to God alone.

41:42-44 And Pharaoh took off his ring from his hand, and put it upon Joseph's hand, and arrayed him in vestures of fine linen, and put a gold chain about his neck; and he made him to ride in the second chariot which he had; and they cried before him, Bow the knee: and he made him ruler over all the land of Egypt. And Pharaoh said unto Joseph, I am Pharaoh, and without thee shall no man lift up his hand or foot in all the land of Egypt.

Pharaoh placed his royal signet ring upon the finger that was never pointed accusingly toward anyone. He then arrayed him in a fine linen robe that was much finer than the coat of many colors, much more comfortable than his slave tunic, and a good bit more respectful than his prison garb. Next, a gold chain is placed around the neck that refused to turn the head to look upon Potiphar's wife.

As Prime Minister of Egypt, Joseph rode as second in command in a chariot behind the king. This is the Bible's first mention of the word "chariot." The chariot was the elite Egyptian's form of transportation. All the Egyptians were required to show him obeisance by bowing on their knees as he passed. Assuredly this, too, included Potiphar and his wife.

And you can't help but wonder if Joseph thought this was some sort of fulfillment of the dreams he had thirteen years before in the land of Canaan.

41:45-46 And Pharaoh called Joseph's name Zaphenathpaeah; and he gave him as his wife Asenath, the daughter of Potiphera, priest of On. And Joseph was thirty years old when he stood before Pharaoh, king of Egypt. And Joseph went out from the presence of Pharaoh, and went throughout all the land of Egypt.

It is not recorded that Joseph was ever addressed by his new name, Zaphenathpaeah, which may mean "God speaks, giving life to the world."

Apparently, after being given his new status, he was addressed with the equivalent of "Prime Minister." Joseph's wife was the daughter of a pagan priest. We are not told that she became a believer in the one true God of the Hebrews, but we do know that Joseph raised their two sons to know the Lord God Jehovah.

Joseph knew that he had seven years of diligent work ahead of him. He accomplished the daunting task of surveying all the land of Egypt and making the necessary preparations to ensure its survival.

41:47-49 And in the seven plenteous years the earth brought forth by handfuls. And he gathered up all the food of the seven years, which were in the land of Egypt, and laid up the food in the cities: the food of the field, which was around about every city, laid he up the same. And Joseph gathered grain as the sand of the sea, very much, until he ceased numbering; for it was without number.

41:50-52 And unto Joseph were born two sons before the years of famine came, whom Asenath, the daughter of Potiphera, priest of On, bore unto him. And Joseph called the name of the first-born Manasseh: For God, said he, hath made me forget all my toil, and all my father's house. And the name of the second called he Ephraim: For God hath caused me to be fruitful in the land of my affliction.

Joseph gave his two sons Hebrew names indicating that he had not forgotten his toil or his father's house. In naming his second son, he mentioned being fruitful in the land of his affliction. He's the Prime Minister of a massive land filled with abundance, why did he call it "the land of my affliction?" His words betrayed his inner heart that would never call Egypt home or its people his own. These scriptures give us the first glimpse into his emotions.

NOTE: Two men in scripture were named Manasseh. Joseph's son Manasseh should not be confused with the evil son of Hezekiah, also named Manasseh.

41:53-54 And the seven years of plenteousness, that was in the land of Egypt were ended. And the seven years of famine began to come, according as Joseph had said: and the famine was in all lands; but in all the land of Egypt there was bread.

Yes, drought and crop failures were experienced by the Egyptians, but they had plenty of bread due to God's goodness and Joseph's diligence.

41:55-57 And when all the land of Egypt was famished, the people cried to Pharaoh for bread: and Pharaoh said unto all the Egyptians, Go unto Joseph; what he saith to you do. And the famine was all over the face of the earth. And Joseph opened all the storehouses, and sold unto the Egyptians; and the famine was severe in the land of Egypt. And all countries came into Egypt to Joseph to buy grain; because the famine was so severe in all lands.

By the providence of Jehovah-God, Joseph was used mightily to bless all the Egyptians. God had been leading, guiding, and directing Joseph's life these many years without him being aware. Yes, the journey was rough but not without purpose.

Genesis
Chapter 42

42:1-2 Now when Jacob saw that there was grain in Egypt, Jacob said unto his sons, Why do ye look one upon another? And he said, Behold, I have heard that there is grain in Egypt: get you down there, and buy for us from there; that we may live, and not die.

Our story turns now to Jacob and his eleven sons dwelling in the land of Canaan. It appears that there is no leader among the bunch. They were hungry, and they lacked bread, and, yet no one had the gumption to get up and take action. Jacob had to urge them to go to Egypt to avoid starvation. Perhaps they were reluctant to travel to Egypt knowing that Joseph might be there.

42:3-5 And Joseph's ten brethren went down to buy grain in Egypt. But Benjamin, Joseph's brother, Jacob sent not with his brethren; for he said, Lest perhaps mischief befall him. And the sons of Israel (Jacob) came to buy grain among those that came; for the famine was in the land of Canaan.

Jacob wasn't about to take a chance of something happening to Benjamin as it had his older brother. These two were the last sons born to Jacob. They were full brothers whose mother Rachel had died following Benjamin's birth.

42:6-8 And Joseph was governor over the land, and he it was that sold to all the people of the land: and

Joseph's brethren came, and bowed down themselves before him with their faces to the earth. And Joseph saw his brethren and knew them; but made himself strange unto them, and spoke roughly unto them; and he said unto them, From where come ye? And they said, From the land of Canaan to buy food. And Joseph knew his brethren, but they knew him not.

Ten hungry brothers came and appeared before the governor of Egypt who was probably thirty-nine-years-old and who in no way resembled the seventeen-year-old they had treacherously betrayed. His appearance and speech were totally Egyptian. They had not expected to see their brother again much less to find him in a position of such great power and themselves in such a position of great need. Their unforeseen arrival was quite a shock for Joseph for sure. And, here they are bowing down with their faces to the earth just as his God-given dream had foretold. Joseph wasn't ready to show his true identity; not just yet.

42:9-10 And Joseph remembered the dreams, which he dreamed of them, and said unto them, Ye are spies; to see the nakedness of the land ye are come. And they said unto him, Nay, my lord, but to buy food are thy servants come.

Joseph remembered more than the dreams. He also remembered their betrayal and their animosity. But he wasn't aware of their hatefulness in returning the blood-drenched torn coat of many colors to their grief stricken father.

63

We will understand as this saga continues that Joseph was not being vengeful or vindictive. He was not desiring to punish them. God was using him to skillfully bring them to soul-cleansing repentance.

Throughout our lifetimes, God allows us to experience difficulty that can only be relieved by his intervention. This is one way we are made aware of our need of him, and it is a way he uses to demonstrate his love.

42:11-16 We are all one man's sons; we are true men, thy servants are no spies. And he said unto them, Nay, but, to see the nakedness of the land ye art come. And they said, Thy servants are twelve brethren, the sons of one man in the land of Canaan; and, behold, the youngest is this day with our father, and one is not. And Joseph said unto them, That is it that I spoke unto you saying, Ye are spies. Hereby ye shall be tested: by the life of Pharaoh ye shall not go forth from here, except your youngest brother come here. Send one of you, and let him fetch your brother, and ye shall be kept in prison, that your words may be tested, whether there is any truth in you: or else, by the life of Pharaoh, surely ye are spies.

The one who "is not" knew they "were not" true men, as they had proclaimed. He continued to test their sincerity. By placing them in prison, they were given a small taste of what Joseph had endured. They were falsely accused, put in a foreign prison, and would remain there for an unknown length of time. Sound familiar?

42:17-20 And he put them all together into prison three days. And Joseph said unto them the third day, This do, and live; for I fear God. If ye be true men, let one of your brethren be bound in the house of your prison: go ye, carry grain for the famine of your houses; but bring your youngest brother unto me; so shall your words be verified, and ye shall not die. And they did so.

Perhaps, because he was concerned for his kinsmen living in famine, Joseph limited their stay in prison to three days. At least they were put there together; whereas he had been imprisoned alone among strangers a few years before.

Surprisingly, Joseph told them that he feared Jehovah-God. Did they think it strange that this presumably Egyptian ruler feared the same God they were supposed to fear? No record is given of any of these brothers calling on the name of the Lord or looking to him in any way. Perhaps their guilty consciences prevented them from doing so. You know living with a decades-long guilty conscience would be like having a heart filled with rotted cargo with no place to unload.

Joseph may have required Benjamin be brought to him so he could be certain that Benjamin hadn't met with the same envy and jealousy as he had.

Joseph still needed them to prove that they were "true men." They agreed with his requirement; welcoming the opportunity to get out of prison.

42:21-24 And they said one to another, We are verily guilty concerning our brother, in that we saw the anguish of his soul, when he besought us, and we

65

would not hear; therefore is this distress come upon us. And Reuben answered them saying, Spoke I not unto you, saying, Do not sin against the child; and ye would not hear? Therefore, behold, also his blood is required. And they knew not that Joseph understood them; for he spoke unto them by an interpreter. And he turned himself about from them, and wept; and returned to them again, and spoke with them, and took from them Simeon, and bound him before their eyes.

We are only told now that these brothers had witnessed Joseph's pain their actions caused and that, when he had called out to them, they had refused to hear. Their guilt-ridden memories were coursing through their minds like a deep reservoir of regret.

37:39 records that they had heartlessly sat down to eat bread after taking Joseph's coat of many colors and casting him into the waterless pit. He needed mercy and none was extended.

Joseph hid his weeping from them when he heard their words of remorse as they recalled their evil deeds. They were in a quandary not knowing if God was at last judging them without mercy. One thing is certain, they knew their day of reckoning had arrived. And Joseph knew that, whereas they were sorry for their previous sin, they were not truly repentant. A truly repentant person forsakes his sin. A person who is merely sorry for his sin, or is sorry he was caught, may return to the same sin when given an opportunity.

Just think of how perplexed the interpreter must have been by their words. Another question arises. Why did Joseph choose Simeon to stay behind as security? Understandably, he knew the brothers who portrayed themselves as "true men" could not be trusted.

Jacob had chosen Joseph to be in line to receive the inheritance of the firstborn and to become the tribe's leader, even though he wasn't the firstborn. The actual firstborn, Reuben, was disqualified due to moral impurity. The next up on the totem pole was Simeon, Jacob's second-born son. Joseph, not trusting his brothers, may have been trying to preserve Simeon to become the heir.

Another thought is that Joseph knew Reuben had tried to avert their evil plot against him, whereas, Simeon had participated. Perhaps this was, at least, part of his decision to retain him. To drive home the fact that he had absolute authority over them, Joseph binds Simeon in their presence.

42:25-28 Then Joseph commanded to fill their sacks with grain and to restore every man's money into his sack, and to give them provision for the way: and thus did he unto them. And they loaded their asses with the grain, and departed from there. And as one of them opened his sack to give his ass fodder in the inn, he discovered his money; for, behold, it was in his sack's mouth. And he said unto his brethren, My money is restored; and, lo, it is even in my sack; and they were afraid, saying one to another, What is this that God hath done unto us?

Well, at last they are considering God might have his hand in all of this. A guilty conscience, my friend, will follow you to the grave and beyond unless it's resolved. They think finding the money is an ill token from God and do not perceive that Joseph had intended it to be an added blessing.

42:29-38 And they came unto Jacob their father, unto the land of Canaan, and told him all that befell unto them, saying, The man, who is the lord of the land, spoke roughly to us, and took us for spies of the country. And we said unto him, We are true men; we are no spies. We are twelve brethren, sons of our father; one is not, and the youngest is this day with our father in the land of Canaan. And the man, the lord of the country, said unto us, Hereby shall I know that ye are true men: leave one of your brethren here with me, and take food for the famine of your households, and be gone. And bring your youngest brother unto me; then shall I know that ye are no spies, but that ye are true men: so will I deliver you your brother, and ye shall do business in the land. And it came to pass as they emptied their sacks, that, behold, every man's bundle of money was in his sack: and when both they and their father saw the bundles of money, they were afraid. And Jacob, their father, said unto them, Me have ye bereaved of my children; Joseph is not, and Simeon is not, and ye will take Benjamin away: all these things are against me. And Reuben spoke unto his father, saying, Slay my two sons, if I bring him not to thee again. And he said, My son shall not go down with you; for his brother is dead, and he is left alone: if mischief befall

68

him by the way in the which ye go, then shall ye bring down my gray hairs with sorrow to Sheol.

The entire incidence was told to Jacob who responded by lamenting his own loss and the possibility of further loss. Much to the merit of Reuben, he offered the lives of his two sons if even more sorrow comes upon his father. This doesn't mean that Reuben would forfeit the lives of his two sons. This statement proved his determination to bring both Simeon and Benjamin home.

Jacob resolutely declared that he won't send Benjamin down to Egypt. Even with the still-present threat of famine, he would rather leave Simeon in an Egyptian prison than to risk losing Benjamin. Hmmm.

Genesis
Chapter 43

43:1-6 And the famine was severe in the land. And it came to pass, when they had eaten up the grain which they had brought out of Egypt, their father said unto them, Go again, buy us a little food. And Judah spoke unto him, saying, The man did solemnly protest unto us, saying, Ye shall not see my face, except your brother be with you. If thou wilt send our brother with us, we will go down and buy food; But if thou wilt not send him, we will not go down; for the man said unto us, Ye shall not see my face, except your brother be with you. And Israel (Jacob) said, Wherefore dealt ye so ill with me, as to tell the man whether ye had yet a brother?

Jacob would not make a move until the famine forced him. He asked his sons to return to Egypt and "buy us a little food." They did not know how long the famine would last. What amount of food would it take to sustain this entourage for an unknown amount of time? Still, Jacob was determined to only purchase the bare minimum.

Throughout this saga, Reuben and Judah were the only sons who reasoned with their father. Jacob seems to have always spoken as though he personally was the victim. But he never blamed his God. He asked a question that needed to be answered. Why had they let it be known that they had another brother?

43:7 And they said, The man asked us carefully of our state, and of our kindred, saying, Is your father yet alive?

Have ye another brother? And we told him according to the tenor of these words. Could we certainly know that he would say, Bring your brother down?

The use of the word "tenor," a Hebrew word (#6310) meaning "command," lets us know that Joseph spoke with an authority that these brothers respected and dared not challenge.

Genesis 43:8-10 And Judah said unto Israel, his father, Send the lad with me, and we will arise and go, that we may live, and not die, both we, and thou, and also our little ones. I will be surety for him; of my hand shalt thou require him: if I bring him not unto thee, and set him before thee, then let me bear the blame forever; for except we had lingered, surely now we had returned this second time.

Judah spoke words that caused his father to understand that he wasn't the only one affected by this dire dilemma. He was saying, "If our younger brother is not brought down to Egypt, we will all die of starvation. If you had let us go when we wanted to, this whole affliction would have been a thing of the past by now."
Leave it to Judah to reason out an agreeable compromise just as he did when he suggested that the brothers profit from selling Joseph as a slave rather than merely leaving him to die of thirst or to be eaten by a beast.
Now that the life of everyone in their tribe was on the line, he was willing to be surety for Benjamin. Desperate people do desperate things. Like Reuben, Judah is now

willing to accept blame and disgrace should their mission fail. It's curious that no one expressed concern for Simeon. An unknown amount of time had passed since they left him alone and in prison.

43:11-14 And their father, Israel, said unto them, If it must be so now, do this: take of the best fruits in the land in your vessels, and carry down the man a present, a little balm, and a little honey, spices, and myrrh, nuts, and almonds. And take double money in your hand; and the money that was brought again in the mouth of your sacks, carry it again in your hand; perhaps it was an oversight. Take also your brother and go unto the man; and God Almighty give you mercy before the man, that he may send away your other brother, and Benjamin. If I am bereaved of my children, I am bereaved.

Israel (Jacob) surrendered to the inevitable. He gave their best preserved fruits and portions of the remaining food supply. Their stored grain, and the Egyptian grain bought earlier had been consumed.

Joseph has thus far been described as "the man" nine times. He will only be identified as "the man" one more time before something mind-boggling occurs.

43:15 And the men took that present, and they took double money in their hand, and Benjamin; and rose up, and went down into Egypt, and stood before Joseph.

No insight into their thoughts, emotions, or intentions was given as they left their father and returned a second time to Egypt. Between verses 15 and 16 is the whole span of time from Canaan's land to standing before Joseph.

43:16-18 And when Joseph saw Benjamin with them, he said to the ruler of his house, Bring these men home, and slaughter an animal, and make ready; for these men shall dine with me at noon. And the man did as Joseph ordered; and the man brought the men into Joseph's house. And the men were afraid, because they were brought into Joseph's house; and they said, Because of the money that was returned in our sacks at the first time are we brought in; that he may seek occasion against us, and fall upon us, and take us for slaves, and our asses.

Joseph was deeply affected by seeing Benjamin alive and well. The brothers do not understand the Egyptian language Joseph used to instruct his servant. He sought to bless his brothers with a hearty meal, but they are too guilt ridden to believe such good fortune. They were worried over the possibility of becoming Egyptian slaves, yet they had not been worried about Joseph becoming a one. Interesting.
They must have arrived sometime early in the morning since the meal was to be served at noon.

43:19-23 And they came near to the steward of Joseph's house, and they spoke with him at the door of the house, and said, O, sir, we came indeed down at the first time to buy food; and it came to pass, when we came to the inn, that we opened our sacks, and behold, every man's money was in the mouth of his sack, our money in full weight: and we have brought it again in our hand. And other money have we brought down in our hands to buy food: we cannot tell you who put our money in our sacks. And he said, Peace be to you, fear not, your God, and the God of your father, hath given you treasure in your sacks: I had your money. And he brought Simeon out unto them.

The brothers were greatly disturbed, but evidently felt at ease sharing their deep concerns to the servant. This unnamed steward of Joseph's house was an intriguing person. Why would he comfort these ten foreign men by saying, "Peace be to you, fear not, your God, and the God of your father, hath given you treasure in your sacks; I had your money?" He knew they had no peace, so he said, "peace." He knew they were racked with fear, so he said, "fear not." He graciously cleared up the mystery of their money by saying, "I had your money." But, best of all, he expressed confidence in the God of the Hebrews. Had he observed Joseph's faithfulness to God? The word used for "God" is the same Hebrew word (H-430) found throughout Joseph's saga. This Egyptian servant who spoke well in the Hebrew language had been sovereignly placed in Joseph's life and in the life of his brothers.

43:24-28 And the man brought the men into Joseph's house, and gave them water, and they washed their feet; and he gave their asses fodder. And they made ready the present for Joseph's coming at noon; for they heard that they should eat bread there. And when Joseph came home, they brought him the present which was in their hand into the house, and bowed themselves to him to the earth. And he asked them of their welfare, and said, Is your father well, the old man of whom ye spoke? Is he yet alive? And they answered, Thy servant, our father, is in good health, he is yet alive. And they bowed down their heads, and made obeisance.

Joseph may have experienced a few mental flashbacks as he saw and smelled the delicacies spread on the dinner table for his enjoyment. Possibly the last time he smelled the fragrance of spices, myrrh, and balm from Canaan land was as he was engulfed in them while being carried off to be auctioned as a slave. The gifts they brought to show good will may have reminded him of their cruelty.

The brothers were so overwhelmed by the uncertainty of what was happening that they overlooked some important clues. Why does this Egyptian show such interest in their father? Why does he speak openly of the Hebrew God, the great God Jehovah? Why had he, at first, spoken roughly to them accusing them of being spies? Why, after putting them in prison for three days, does he now invite them to dinner?

Verse 28 marks the third time the brothers have bowed their heads and made obeisance to the one whom they had mocked and scorned and sold to be a slave. Joseph's dream that became a nightmare had become a reality right before his eyes. He knew that he did not direct this circumstance. Who but God could have orchestrated the fulfillment of his dreams? And, the purposes of God are still a long way from being fulfilled.

43:29-30 And he lifted up his eyes and saw his brother Benjamin, his mother's son, and said, Is this your younger brother, of whom ye spoke unto me? And he said, God be gracious unto thee, my son. And Joseph made haste; for his heart yearned over his brother; and he sought where to weep; and he entered into his chamber, and wept there.

Looking beyond the gifts, Joseph had to ask if this was his full-brother Benjamin. These brothers would have to have been klutzes not to wonder about this man who pronounced a blessing upon their younger brother. Overcome by emotion, Joseph sought solitude to hide his masquerade. Throughout these perplexing years, Joseph had had no one to confide in, no one to share his anguish and disappointment, and no one to help him comprehend that that God had ordained him to preserve his posterity.

43:31-33 And he washed his face, and went out, and controlled himself, and said, Set on bread. And they set on for him by himself, and for them by themselves, and for the Egyptians, who did eat with him, by themselves: because the Egyptians might not eat bread with the Hebrews; for that is an abomination unto the Egyptians. And they sat before him, the first-born according to his birthright, and the youngest according to his youth: and the men marveled one at another.

Well, glory! These fellas were beginning to marvel.

43:34 And he took and sent messes unto them from before him: but Benjamin's mess was five times as much as any of theirs. And they drank, and were merry with him.

Joseph tested the brothers by this unexplained show of favoritism.

Genesis
Chapter 44

44:1-6 And he commanded the steward of his house, saying, Fill the men's sacks with food, as much as they can carry, and put every man's money in his sack's mouth. And put my cup, the silver cup, in the sack's mouth of the youngest, and his grain money. And he did according to the word that Joseph had spoken. As soon as the morning was light, the men were sent away, they and their asses. And when they were gone out of the city, and not yet far off, Joseph said unto his steward, Up, follow after the men; and when thou dost overtake them, say unto them, Wherefore have ye rewarded evil for good? Is not this it in which my lord drinketh, and whereby indeed he divineth? Ye have done evil in so doing. And he overtook them, and he spoke unto them these same words.

This is where this soup thickened instantly. Joseph's living standard in Egypt was very high indeed and included drinking out of a silver cup. He did not "divine" as this was would involve pagan religious practices. Joseph may have used this to disguise his true identify and to cause the brothers to think he knew all about them, which, of course he did.

The brothers got a taste of what it was to be in a strange and to be wrongfully accused. They had begun to reap what they had sown.

44:7-9 And they said unto him, Wherefore saith my lord these words? God forbid that thy servants should do according to this thing: Behold, the money, which we found in our sacks' mouths, we brought again unto thee out of the land of Canaan, How, then, should we steel out of thy lord's house silver or gold? With whomsoever of thy servants it be found, both let him die, and we will also be my lord's slaves.

Horrified at the accusation, the brothers proclaimed their innocence asking why they would steal a silver cup when they had plenty of money to buy one should they desire it. They sealed their doom with the promise that, should one of them have stolen the silver cup, he would be executed and the others made slaves. Those words would be shortly regretted.

44:10-13 And he said, Now also let it be according unto your words: he with whom it is found shall be my servant; and ye shall be blameless. Then they speedily took down every man his sack to the ground, and opened every man his sack. And he searched and began at the eldest, and ceased at the youngest: and the cup was found in Benjamin's sack. Then they tore their clothes, and loaded every man his ass, and returned to the city.

As they have dealt treacherously in the past, so it has returned upon their heads. They could have continued on without the young Benjamin but they would have to face their father. To their merit, they returned to Joseph's house where Judah acted as spokesman.

44:14-17 And Judah and his brethren came to Joseph's house for he was yet there: and they fell before him on the ground. And Joseph said unto them, What deed is this that ye have done? Know ye not that such a man as I can divine? And Judah said, What shall we say unto my lord? What shall we speak? Or how shall we clear ourselves? God hath found out the iniquity of thy servants: behold, we are my lord's servants, both we, and he also with whom the cup is found. And he said, God forbid that I should do so: but the man in whose hand the cup is found, he shall be my servant; and as for you, get you up in peace unto your father.

As a ray of light began to expose Judah's guilty heart, he lamented, "God hath found out the iniquity of thy servants." Perhaps his heart was the heaviest since he was the one who suggested Joseph's coat of many colors be dipped in goat's blood and given to their father.

Just as Judah had been the one to reason with their father, he will now be the one to reason with Joseph. His heart-rending dialog was unrehearsed. He spoke well considering that he and the brothers were in a total state of shock as this event unfolded.

44:18-23 Then Judah came near unto him, and said, O my lord, let thy servant, I pray thee, speak a word in my lord's ears, and let not thine anger burn against thy servant; for thou art even as Pharaoh. My lord asked his servants, saying, Have ye a father, or a brother? And we said unto my lord, We have a father, an old man, and a child of his old age, a little one; and his brother is dead, and he alone is left of his mother; and his father loveth him. And thou saidst unto thy servants, Bring him down unto me, that I may set my eyes upon him. And we said unto my lord, The lad cannot leave his father; for if he should leave his father, his father would die. And thou saidst unto thy servants, Except your youngest brother came down with you, ye shall see my face no more.

44:24-31 And it came to pass when we came up unto thy servant, my father, we told him the words of my lord. And our father said, Go again, and buy us a little food. And we said, We cannot go down: if our youngest brother be with us, then we will go down; for we may not see the man's face, except our youngest brother be with us. And thy servant, my father, said unto us, Ye know that my wife bore me two sons; And the one went from me, and I said, Surely, he is torn in pieces; and I saw him not since. And if ye take this also from me, and mischief befall him, ye shall bring down my gray hairs with sorrow to the grave (Sheol.) Now therefore when I come to thy servant, my father, and the lad is not with us; seeing that his life is bound up in the lad's life; It shall come to pass, when he seeth that the lad is not with us, that he will die: and thy servants shall bring down the gray hairs of thy servant, our father, with sorrow to the grave (Sheol).

Compassion for his father that wasn't there before has now surfaced. Could this have been what some of the testing was about?

44:32-34 For thy servant became surety for the lad unto my father, saying, If I bring him not unto thee, then I shall bear the blame to my father forever. Now therefore, I pray thee, let thy servant abide instead of the lad a slave to my lord; and let the lad go up with his brethren. For how shall I go up to my father, and the lad is not with me? Lest perhaps I see the evil that shall come on my father.

Judah rather eloquently rehearsed the entire matter before Joseph while the others remained silent. Their hearts must have been tremendously stirred as the history was given. Judah did not proclaim Benjamin's innocence. Neither did he bring an accusation against any Egyptian. Of course, everyone knew it didn't get in Benjamin's stuff by itself. The brothers now knew what it was to be treated maliciously.

And Joseph now knew that Judah's heart had been changed and that he was not the same man he was twenty-two years ago. Judah's speech-like confession was music to his ears. And he acknowledged that Joseph "is as Pharaoh;" meaning he was as a god. This doesn't mean that Joseph wanted to be thought of as a god.

Genesis
Chapter 45

45:1-8 Then Joseph could not control himself before all them who stood by him; and he cried, Cause every man to go out from me. And there stood no man with him, while Joseph made himself known unto his brethren. And he wept aloud: and the Egyptians and the house of Pharaoh heard. And Joseph said unto his brethren, <u>I am Joseph; doth my father yet live</u>? And his brethren could not answer him; for they were terrified at his presence. And Joseph said unto his brethren, Come near me, I pray you. And they came near. And he said, I am Joseph your brother, whom ye sold into Egypt. Now therefore be not grieved, nor angry with yourselves, that ye sold me here; for God did send me before you to preserve life. For these two years hath the famine been in the land: and yet there are five years, in which there shall neither be plowing or harvest. And God sent me before you to preserve you a posterity in the earth, and to save your lives by a great deliverance. So now it was not you that sent me here, but God: and he hath made me a father to Pharaoh, and lord of all his house, and a ruler throughout all the land of Egypt.

NOTE: Jesus' brethren didn't recognize him the first time, but they will at his second coming.
Zechariah 12:10 ... and they shall look upon me whom they have pierced, and they shall mourn ...)

As Joseph's heart burst, the first words he spoke were, "<u>I am Joseph; doth my father yet live</u>?" The brothers were too stunned to speak. He invited them to come near to him in order to examine him more closely. He cautioned them to not be angry or grieved with themselves as he acknowledged that he now understood that it was God who had sent him to the spot where they all stood.

God sometimes uses the evil directed by others to the benefit of those who love him in order that it will serve his greater purpose.

Romans 8:28 admonishes believers with these words: And we know that all things work together for good to them that love God, to them who are the called according to his purpose.

Three times Joseph declared that it was God who sent him to Egypt. He tenderly diverted blame from his brothers. Joseph had nothing but good will in his heart toward them.

Beginning with Abraham, Psalm 105 outlines the covenant history of God with his people. Discern the beautiful truth written in:

Psalm 105:17-22 He (God) sent <u>a man</u> before them, even Joseph, who was sold for a servant, whose feet they hurt with fetters; he was laid in iron, until the time that his word came; <u>the word of the Lord tested him</u>. The king sent and loosed him, even the ruler of the people, and let him go free. He made him lord of his house, and ruler of all his substance, to bind his princes at his pleasure, and to teach his elders wisdom.

I tremble at the thought of what the result of my being so severely tested would be. How I admire this man Joseph!

Psalm 81:5 This he ordained in Joseph for a testimony, when he went out through the land of Egypt, where I heard a language that I understood not.

Joseph acknowledged that "God sent me before you to preserve you a posterity in the earth." **(Genesis 45:7)** The word, "posterity" is interesting, but it can be overlooked by only a casual glance. This Hebrew word (#7611) means "to remain, reserve, remnant, to be left." Joseph appreciated that God had strategically placed him in a position to preserve his people. In Joseph's limited vision, his concern was for the preservation of his immediate family. As you know, God's purposes are high above our understanding. He had purposed to preserve a people unto himself.

Let's make a special note: When Joseph said that God had made him a father unto Pharaoh, he was referring to a new and younger Pharaoh other than the one whom he had dealt with previously. This new Pharaoh was Senusert III who reigned from 1878-1841 B.C.

45:9-15 Haste ye, and go up to my father, and say unto him, Thus saith thy son, Joseph: God hath made me lord of all Egypt; come down unto me, tarry not; and thou shalt dwell in the land of Goshen, and thou shalt be near unto me, thou, and thy children, and thy children's children, and thy flocks, and thy herds, and all that thou hast. And there will I nourish thee; for yet there are five years of famine; lest thou, and thy household, and all that thou hast, come to poverty. And, behold, your eyes see, and the eyes of my brother, Benjamin, that it is my mouth that speaketh unto you. And ye shall tell my father of all my glory in Egypt, and of all that ye have seen; and ye shall haste and bring down my father here. And he fell upon his brother Benjamin's neck, and wept; and Benjamin wept upon his neck. Moreover, he kissed all his brethren, and wept upon them; and <u>after that his brethren talked with him.</u>

Joseph didn't need any more evidence of his brothers' hearts being changed. Do you remember in the beginning, the scripture said that they hated him so much that they could not speak unto him peaceably? (**37:4**) But now, after forgiveness has flowed from the throne of God down through their hearts, they wept (meaning a loud lamentation) together and <u>his brethren talked with him</u>!

Well, it's time to shout, "Glory hallelujah. And praise God!" That talk must have been quite a talk! They had a lot of catching up to do.

Joseph knew the Hebrew monotheistic belief and customs were not compatible with the Egyptians. By God's grace, he had lived in Egypt and yet had not been corrupted by their pagan beliefs and lifestyles. He told his brothers that the land of Goshen would be suitable for livestock and grain, and would be designated as a safe haven for them.

The Nile River, the world's longest river, flows from south to north some 4,135 miles. The land of Goshen was located in the delta area at the northern end. This separated them from the main cities of Egypt and kept them from being corrupted by pagan lifestyles. God had made a way to preserve a people for his own.

45:16-20 and the report thereof was heard in Pharaoh's house, saying, Joseph's brethren are come: and it pleased Pharaoh well, and his servants. And Pharaoh said unto Joseph, Say unto thy brethren, This do ye; load your beasts, and go, get you unto the land of Canaan; and take your father and your households, and come unto me; and I will give you the good of the land of Egypt, and ye shall eat the fat of the land. Now thou art commanded, this do ye: take your wagons out of the land of Egypt for your little ones, and for your wives, and bring your father, and come. Also regard not your stuff (furniture) for the good of all the land of Egypt is yours.

Wow! This is what's called "highly favored." It was Pharaoh who commanded Joseph's entire family to come to Egypt, and he generously pledged they could enjoy "all the good of the land." Not a bad deal. Pharaoh and the Hebrews are all thinking that they will be there only for the five years remaining of the famine. Actually, this five year expectation would become a 430 year reality. **(Exodus 12:40)**

45:21-24 And the children of Israel did so; and Joseph gave them wagons, according to the commandment of Pharaoh, and gave them provision for the way. To all of them he gave each man changes of raiment; but to

Benjamin he gave three hundred pieces of silver, and five changes of raiment. And to his father he sent after this manner: ten asses loaded with the good things of Egypt, and ten she-asses loaded with grain and meat and bread for his father by the way. So he sent his brethren away, and they departed; and he said unto them, See that ye fall not out of the way.

It's not clear why Joseph continued to favor Benjamin so obviously. But the brethren weren't concerned with favoritism any more. They realized that an extraordinary amount of grace has been extended to them resulting in reconciliation forgiveness, and cleansing. Knowing his brothers, Joseph warned, "See that ye fall not out by the way." He knew there would be time enough on the three-day journey back to Canaan's land to have fears and doubts torment their minds. He cautioned that there be no strife or quarreling among them.

Before we study the next verses, let's stop and consider that we aren't told that Joseph ever gave an explanation to his brothers as to why he spoke "roughly" to them in the beginning, why he put them through the ordeal with finding money in their sacks, why he put them in prison three days, and then later came the episode of finding the silver cup. They may have realized that this was done to prove them. And they knew by now that they had been proven.

Now the brothers are going to face their father. The joy of knowing that Joseph is alive, that his blood is not on their hands, that they have been forgiven, that they have been assured of ample provision for the remainder of the famine may have been eclipsed by the dread of confessing to their father the evil they had perpetrated against Joseph and the guilt they felt at having caused their father to live in deep anguish and grief. If this had been their dread, it vanished when Jacob accepted the news without questioning.

45:25-28 And they went up out of Egypt, and came into the land of Canaan unto Jacob, their father, and told him, saying, Joseph is yet alive, and he is governor over all the land of Egypt. And Jacob's heart fainted; for he believed them not. And they told him all the words of Joseph, which he had said unto them; and when he saw the wagons which Joseph had sent to carry him, the spirit of Jacob, their father, revived: and Israel said, it is enough: Joseph my son is yet alive; I will go and see him before I die.

Jacob was 130 years old when he arrived in Egypt thinking he would "go and see my son" before he died. God saw to it that he not only saw Joseph, but he lived another seventeen years in Goshen and saw Joseph's sons too.

Genesis
Chapter 46

46:1-4 And Israel (Jacob) took his journey with all that he had, and came to Beer-Sheba, and offered sacrifices unto the God of his father Isaac, and God spoke unto Israel in the visions of the night, and said, Jacob, Jacob. And he said, I am God, the God of thy father; fear not to go down into Egypt; for I will make of thee a great nation. I will go down with thee into Egypt; and I will surely bring thee up again; and Joseph shall put his hand upon your eyes.

No doubt that Jacob's heart was deeply troubled as he left the land that God had promised to give his people. Many questions and fears saturated his heart and mind. Not wanting to be disobedient to God, as an act of faith, he went to Beer-Sheba to sacrifice.

You may wonder, "Why Beer-Sheba? He could have sacrificed anywhere." His choosing to sacrifice is significant in itself. His choosing to go to Beer-Sheba is even more significant because that is where his father Abraham planted a tamarisk tree as a reminder of his treaty made there with Abimelech, and he called upon the name of the Everlasting God (**Genesis 21:33**.) Beer-Sheba literally means, "the well of the oath."

God had appeared to Abraham's son Isaac at Beer-Sheba and confirmed that the promises made to his father were also his (**Genesis 26:23-25**.) "I am the God of your father Abraham, do not fear, for I am with you, I will bless you and multiply your descendants."

When God speaks, "I am with you," he eliminates all fear and concern. This same God who said, "I am with you," to Abraham, Isaac, and Jacob also spoke the same words to Jeremiah (**Jeremiah 1:8,19**.) And, in **Acts 18:10**, we read these words spoken by God to Paul at Corinth, "Be not afraid, but speak, and hold not thy peace; for I am with thee ..."

Throughout the remainder of his lifetime, Jacob would hold to God's promise, "I will bring thee up again." He was not to fear as he "took his journey." God had assured him that he was in his will and that he would go with him and there fulfill his promise to make of him a great nation.

God was careful to assure him that "Joseph shall put his hand upon your eyes," signifying that his beloved Joseph would be by his side at the moment of his death.

Yes, Jacob was eager to see his beloved Joseph, but he was more eager to be assured that by journeying to Egypt he would be in God's will.

46:5-7 And Jacob rose up from Beer-Sheba; and the sons of Israel carried Jacob, their father, and their little ones, and their wives, in the wagons which Pharaoh had sent to carry him. And they took their cattle, and their goods, which they had gotten in the land of Canaan, and came into Egypt, Jacob, and all his seed with him. His sons, and his sons' sons with him, his daughters, and his sons' daughters, and all his seed brought he with him into Egypt.

Let's read more scriptures from **Psalm 105:** where we learned earlier that it was God who had sent Joseph into Egypt.

Verses 23-24 tell us that God did indeed fulfill his promise to his people:

"Israel (Jacob) also came into Egypt, and Jacob sojourned in the land of Ham. And he increased his people greatly, and made them stronger than their enemies."

Genesis 46:8-27 is a listing of names that provide a history

46:8 This scripture begins with, "And these are the names of the children of Israel," which is the first time the author, Moses, refers to the family as a whole.

46:9-27 These scriptures list the names of the seventy people who went down to Egypt.

46:28-30 And he sent Judah before him unto Joseph, to direct his face unto Goshen; and they came into the land of Goshen. And Joseph made ready his chariot, and went up to meet Israel, his father, to Goshen, and presented himself unto him; and he fell on his neck, and wept on his neck a good while. And Israel said unto Joseph, Now let me die, since I have seen thy face, because thou art yet alive.

Joseph, as Prime Minister of Egypt, had his own chariot which was drawn by four horses. It wasn't at all like the Midianite's wagon he was carried in when he arrived as a slave.

Scripture doesn't tell us if Jacob asked why Joseph had not contacted him, why he had adopted the Egyptian appearance and speech, or asked if he had remained faithful to the God of his fathers. All questions in his heart were settled at his first glance of his beloved son.

46:31-34 And Joseph said unto his brethren, and unto his father's house, I will go up, and show Pharaoh, and say unto him, My brethren, and my father's house, who were in the land of Canaan, are come unto me; and the men are shepherds, for their trade hath been to feed cattle; and they have brought their flocks, and their herds, and all that they have. And it shall come to pass, when Pharaoh shall call you, and shall say, what is your occupation? That ye shall say, Thy servants' trade hath been about cattle from our youth even until now, both we, and also our fathers; that ye may dwell in the land of Goshen; for every shepherd is an abomination unto the Egyptians.

Joseph wanted to make sure that they would be permitted to remain in the land of Goshen, so he counseled them on what to say and what not to say.

Genesis
Chapter 47

47:1-6 Then Joseph came and told Pharaoh, and said, My father and my brethren, and their flocks, and their herds, and all that they have, are come out of the land of Canaan; and, behold, they are in the land of Goshen. And he took some of his brethren, even five men, and presented them unto Pharaoh. And Pharaoh said unto his brethren, What is your occupation? And they said unto Pharaoh, Thy servants are shepherds, both we, and also our fathers. They said moreover unto Pharaoh, For to sojourn in the land are we come; for thy servants have no pasture for their flocks; for the famine is sore in the land of Canaan: now therefore, we pray thee, let thy servants dwell in the land of Goshen. And Pharaoh spoke unto Joseph saying, Thy father and thy brethren are come unto thee: The land of Egypt is before thee; in the best of the land make thy father and brethren to dwell; in the land of Goshen let them dwell: and if thou knowest any men of activity among them, then make them rulers over my cattle.

Joseph reported the arrival of his family to Pharaoh. We are not told which five brothers he chose to present to Pharaoh, but it may have been Reuben, Judah, and Benjamin among them. As they had been previously instructed by Joseph, they answered wisely saying they were shepherds (of cattle).

In gratitude to Joseph, Pharaoh offered them the best of the land and even offered employment as herdsmen over his cattle.

47:7-10 And Joseph brought in Jacob his father, and set him before Pharaoh: and Jacob blessed Pharaoh. And Pharaoh said unto Jacob, How old art thou? And Jacob said unto Pharaoh, The days of the years of my pilgrimage are an hundred and thirty years: few and evil have the days of the years of my life been, and have not attained unto the days of the years of the life of my fathers in the days of their pilgrimage. And Jacob blessed Pharaoh, and went out from before him.

The aged, partially blind, and possibly invalid Jacob is set before Pharaoh as though he was too infirm to stand. These scriptures say twice that Jacob "blessed Pharaoh," demonstrating that he greeted him with a salutation acknowledging his gratitude. He didn't introduce himself as Pharaoh's "servant" as his sons had.

Perhaps surprised by his appearance, Pharaoh asked his age. Jacob replied that he was an hundred and thirty years old and that his days have been "few and evil," meaning few in comparison to his fathers' days, and "evil" in that they had been filled with struggle and hardship. He thanked Pharaoh again without pointing out that had it not been for his son, Joseph, all of Egypt would be as bad off as the other surrounding countries.

47:11-13 And Joseph placed his father and his brethren, and gave them a possession in the land of Egypt, in the best of the land of Rameses, as Pharaoh commanded. And Joseph nourished his father, and his brethren, and all his father's household, with bread, according to their families. And there was no bread in all the land of Egypt; for the famine was very severe, so that the land of Egypt and all the land of Canaan fainted by reason of the famine.

What is called "the land of Rameses" is the same area known as the land of Goshen. They were placed there by the command of Pharaoh. The "command of Pharaoh" was actually the providence of God. By this means, God had prevented their intermarrying with pagans in the land of Canaan, from learning heathen customs, and from departing from him.

They were given bread "according to their families," meaning their food supply was rationed according to the number in their household. While others were facing starvation, God's people were being nourished by the foresight and means of provision God had given Joseph.

47:14-17 And Joseph gathered up all the money that was found in the land of Egypt, and in the land of Canaan, for the grain which they bought; and Joseph brought the money into Pharaoh's house. And when money failed in the land of Egypt, and in the land of Canaan, all the Egyptians came unto Joseph, and said, Give us bread; for why should we die in thy presence? For the money faileth. And Joseph said, give your cattle; and I will give you for your cattle, if money fail. And they brought their cattle unto Joseph, and Joseph gave them bread in exchange for horses, and for the flocks, and for the cattle of the herds, and for the asses; and he fed them with bread for all their cattle for that year.

The first sentence in verse 14 needs to be carefully read to understand that Joseph began selling the stored grain to the people in Egypt and Canaan. Joseph did not horde the money for himself; instead, he brought all the money into Pharaoh's house. Then, when their money became useless, the Egyptians and Canaanites came to Joseph literally begging for bread. Joseph began giving them bread in exchange for their livestock.

47:18-20 When that year was ended, they came unto him the second year, and said unto him, We will not hide it from my lord, how our money is spent. My lord also hath our herds of cattle; there is not anything left in the sight of my lord, but our bodies, and our lands. Wherefore shall we die before thine eyes, both we and our lands? Buy us and our land for bread, and we and our land will be servants unto Pharaoh; and give us seed, that we may live, and not die, that the land be not desolate. And Joseph bought all the land of Egypt for Pharaoh; for the Egyptians sold every man his field, because the famine prevailed over them: so the land became Pharaoh's.

He purchased the Egyptians' land for Pharaoh's possession and not for his own. This time Joseph was asked not only for bread but for seed also. This indicates that the people believed Joseph's prediction of a seven year famine, and their belief that the famine was coming to a close.

47:21-23 And as for the people, he removed them to cities from one end of the borders of Egypt even to the other end thereof. Only the land of the priests bought he not; for the priests had a portion assigned them by

97

Pharaoh, and did eat their portion which Pharaoh gave them: wherefore they sold not their lands. Then Joseph said unto the people, Behold, I have bought you this day and your land for Pharaoh; lo, here is seed for you, and ye shall sow the land.

Gathering the people into the cities made their survival and the grain distribution manageable. Pharaoh had given land allotments and provided income to their pagan priests. The considered-sacred geese and oxen were provided daily for their consumption. Joseph prudently left this custom as he had found it.

Joseph spoke these words of faith and the people believed them, "ye shall sow the land." Because his words were believed, hope began to grow in their hearts before the seeds began to grow in ground.

47:24-26 (Joseph continued to encourage the people.) And it shall come to pass in the increase (harvest) that ye shall give the fifth part unto Pharaoh, and four parts shall be your own, for seed of the field, and for your food, and for them of your households, and for food for your little ones. And they said, Thou hast saved our lives: let us find grace in the sight of my lord, and we will be Pharaoh's servants. And Joseph made it a law over the land of Egypt unto this day, that Pharaoh should have the fifth part; except the land of the priests only, which became not Pharaoh's.

What thoughts did Joseph have as his words left his mouth? He must have realized that God was speaking through him giving assurance to these people. Yet, he doesn't mention God as he did when he interpreted Pharaoh's dreams years before.

Joseph spoke to them of a harvest and plans for their future well-being when the reality of their existence didn't reflect a hint of it. The people honored and trusted Joseph realizing that he had their best interest at heart. He was not attempting to win their loyalties for himself, and they knew it even though they credited Joseph with saving their lives. According to Joseph's word, they were to give twenty percent of their earned income to Pharaoh. Joseph, the formerly left-for-dead boy, who was sold as a slave, then became a falsely accused prisoner, now had the authority to make the law of the land. Utterly amazing.

47:27-31 And Israel dwelt in the land of Egypt, in the country of Goshen; and they had possessions therein, and grew, and multiplied exceedingly. And Jacob lived in the land of Egypt seventeen years: so the whole age of Jacob was an hundred forty and seven years. And the time drew near that Israel must die; and he called his son, Joseph, and said unto him, If now I have found grace in thy sight, put, I pray thee, thy hand under my thigh, and deal kindly and truly with me; bury me not, I pray thee, in Egypt. But I will lie with my fathers, and thou shalt carry me out of Egypt, and bury me in their burying place. And he said, I will do as thou hast said. And he said, Swear unto me. And he swore unto him. And Israel bowed himself upon the bed's head.

Remember how decrepit Jacob was when he first arrived seventeen years earlier? Here, at the time of his death, he is a hundred forty seven years old and even frailer. Just as the Body of Christ is in the world but not a part of it, Jacob was in Egypt but not a part of it. He trusted Joseph to "deal kindly and truly" in performing his final request to be buried in the Cave of Machpelah (the Cave of the Patriarchs) in the land of Canaan near Hebron. This the cave where Abraham and Sarah, Isaac and Rebecca, and Jacob's wife Leah are buried.

Genesis
Chapter 48

48:1-6 And it came to pass after these things, that one told Joseph, Behold, thy father is sick: and he took with him his two sons, Manasseh and Ephraim. And one told Jacob, and said, Behold, thy son, Joseph, cometh unto thee; and Israel strengthened himself, and sat upon the bed. And Jacob said unto Joseph, God Almighty appeared unto me at Luz in the land of Canaan, and blessed me, and said unto me, Behold, I will make thee fruitful, and multiply thee, and I will make of thee a multitude of people; and will give this land to thy seed after thee for an everlasting possession. And now thy two sons, Ephraim and Manasseh, who were born unto thee in the land of Egypt before I came unto thee in Egypt, are mine; as Reuben and Simeon, they shall be mine. And thy issue, which thou begettest after them, shall be thine, and shall be called after the name of their brethren in their inheritance.

Joseph, sensing his father was sick unto death, had brought his two sons with him to his bedside.

Jacob stated the words spoken to him by God and recorded in **Genesis 35:6**. Though he didn't live to see the fulfillment of God's promise to him, he, nonetheless, believed his word.

Jacob stated that just as Reuben and Simeon were his firstborn sons, he will now adopt Joseph's two firstborn sons as his own. This adoption elevated them to a full tribal inheritance which meant Joseph would have a double portion among his brethren. With this having been done, Joseph's sons never return to their former life in Egypt. Given this new status among their family, they chose to remain in Goshen.

48:7 And as for me, when I came from Paddan, Rachel, died by me in the land of Canaan in the way, when yet there was but a little way to come into Ephrath: and I buried her there in the way of Ephrath; the same is Bethlehem.

48:8-9 And Israel beheld Joseph's sons, and said, Who are these? And Joseph said unto his father, These are my sons, whom God hath given me in this place. And he said, Bring them here, unto me, and I will bless them.

His eyesight, now having failed, made him unable to distinguish Joseph's sons. Joseph emphasized that his sons were gifts from God.

48:10-11 Now the eyes of Israel were dim for age, so that he could not see. And he brought them near unto him; and he kissed them, and embraced them. And Israel said unto Joseph, I had not thought to see thy face; and, lo, God hath shown me also thy seed.

What a tender moment for Jacob, Joseph, Manasseh, and Ephraim. Their descendants would each become a full tribe. God had far exceeded Jacob's hope. (He will yours too.)

48:12-16 And Joseph brought them out from between his knees, and he bowed himself with his face to the earth. And Joseph took them both, Ephraim in his right hand toward Israel's left hand, and Manasseh in his left hand toward Israel's right hand, and brought them near unto him. And Israel stretched out his right hand, and laid it upon Ephraim's head, who was the younger, and his left hand upon Manasseh's head, guiding his hands knowingly; for Manasseh was the firstborn. And he blessed Joseph, and said, God, before whom my fathers Abraham and Isaac did walk, the God who fed me all my life long unto this day. The Angel who redeemed me from all evil, bless the lads; and let my name be named on them, and the name of my fathers Abraham and Isaac; and let them grow into a multitude in the midst of the earth.

Manasseh and Ephraim were so young that they could stand between their father's knees. Jacob knowingly laid his right hand upon the younger Ephraim's head, and his left hand upon the head of Manasseh. Jacob pronounced a blessing upon Joseph and acknowledged that it was the God who had fed him throughout his life. He also acknowledged that he had been redeemed (delivered) from all evil. He, in no way, declared his own virtue or worthiness.

The King James Version authors chose to capitalize the "A" in Angel, making it a proper noun. Other versions use a lower case "a." I will not offer any speculation, but I have chosen to use the capital "A" as a reflection of my personal belief.

48:17-19 And when Joseph saw that his father laid his right hand upon the head of Ephraim, it displeased him: and he held up his father's hand, to remove it from Ephraim's head unto Manasseh's head. And Joseph said unto his father, Not so, my father: For this is the firstborn; put thy right hand upon his head. And his father refused, and said, I know it, my son, I know it: he also shall become a great people, and he also shall be great: but truly his younger brother shall be greater than he, and his seed shall become a multitude of nations.

Even during Joseph's forced exile, he dreamed of his sons obtaining their rightful place amongst their people. Though he hadn't made this desire known, God directed his posterity. He was understandably disappointed that the firstborn blessing was bestowed upon Ephraim and not on Manasseh. This is the only mention of Joseph expressing disappointment. What a remarkable man!

God follows his own order which many times is not the order of man. He chose the younger Isaac over Ismael. He chose Jacob instead of Esau, Joseph instead of Reuben, and now Ephraim rather than Manasseh. Later Gideon and David were both chosen over their older brothers.

48:20-22 And he blessed them that day, saying, In thee shall Israel bless, saying, God make thee as Ephraim and Manasseh. And Israel said unto Joseph, Behold, I die: but God shall be with you, and bring you again unto the land of your fathers. Moreover, I have given to thee one portion above thy brethren, which I took out of the hand of the Amorite with my sword and with my bow.

Genesis
Chapter 49

As this chapter begins, the dying Jacob is comforted by his twelve sons. The Spirit of Prophesy came upon him and brought fresh oil to this flickering lamp.

The blessings and cursings spoken by Jacob in prophesies were conditional. Some were brought to pass immediately, some in later years, and some are yet to be performed.

The qualities of the sons not only affected their own destinies, but, also, that of future generations. Present actions (good or bad) have future results. Present actions tend to shape the future.

49:1-:2 And Jacob called unto his sons, and said, Gather yourselves together, that I may tell you that which shall befall you in the last days. Gather yourselves together, and hear, ye sons of Jacob; and hearken unto Israel, your father.

This is the Bible's first of eight scriptures mentioning the term "last days," which mean the days prior to the coming of the Lord. Jacob is speaking prophetically. He was not saying that his sons would be living in the "last days." He was saying these things shall befall your posterity (future generations) in the last days.

Remember that it was the Spirit of Prophesy speaking through him and covering a time span from their past, to present, and well into the future.

In verses: **3-7,** he began speaking to his sons in birth order. He addressed Reuben, Simeon, and Levi who had all three sinned deeply and without recorded repentance.

In verse: 3 he told Reuben what could have been his but was fortified by unrepentant sin.

49:3-4 Reuben, thou art my first-born, my might, and the beginning of my strength, the excellency of dignity, and the excellency of power. Unstable as water, thou shalt not excel, because thou wentest up to thy father's bed; then defilest thou it; he went up to my couch.

Through moral weakness, Reuben had not been able to govern himself, therefore the birthright of the firstborn was forfeited.

49:5-7 Simeon and Levi are brethren: instruments of cruelty are in their habitations. O my soul, come not thou unto their secret; unto their assembly, mine honor, be not thou united; for in their anger they slew a man, and in their self-will they hamstrung oxen. Cursed be their anger, for it was fierce, and their wrath, for it was cruel: I will divide them in Jacob, and scatter them in Israel.

(Simeon's and Levi's great sin is not included in our study because it is recorded in Genesis 34: before the story of Joseph was begun in Chapter 37.)

107

Here's a summary of what had happened.

A Hivite named Shechem defiled their only sister, Dinah. These two brothers used their weapons, which were intended for defense, to brutally kill a man and an entire village in revenge for their sister having been defiled. Their actions went beyond justice. Their fierce anger boiled over into vengeful rage.

Scripture tells us that the wrath of man works not the righteousness of God (**James 1:20**.) And **Romans 12:19** declares, "Vengeance is mine; I will repay, saith the Lord." It's in our best interest to leave matters to God.

In **49:6** Jacob expressed his deep anguish over their unbridled anger. By their self-will they hamstrung oxen. It was a common practice to disable an enemy's chariot horses by cutting the tendons behind the heels thus rendering them useless. This was not done on an enemy battlefield, and, it wasn't horses they hamstrung. It was oxen used to work their fields and to carry water. Judah prophesied that they would not remain a unit but would be disbursed throughout the tribes because of their unbridled anger.

The following five verses comprise Jacob's prophesy to Judah. Some of its meaning remains unknown.

49:8-13 Judah, thou art him whom thy brothers shall praise: thy hand shall be in the neck of thine enemies: thy father's children shall bow down before thee. Judah is a lion's whelp: from the prey, my son, thou art gone up: he stooped down, he crouched as a lion, and as an old lion. Who shall rouse him up? The scepter, shall not depart from Judah, nor a lawgiver from between his feet until Shiloh come; and unto him shall the gathering of the people be. Binding his foal unto the vine, and his ass' colt unto the choice vine, he washed his garments in wine, and his clothes in the blood of grapes. His eyes shall be red with wine, and his teeth white with milk.

Like Reuben and Simeon, Judah sinned greatly (**Genesis 38,**) and in the matter of his treatment of the young Joseph in that he suggested they "profit" by selling him rather than by merely killing him. However, unlike Reuben and Simeon, he repented, changed his behavior, and was rewarded.

"Until Shiloh come" refers to the coming of the Messiah Jesus. "Shiloh" means rest-giver which, of course, Jesus is.

49:14-15 Issachar is a strong ass crouching down between two burdens; And he saw that the rest was good, and the land that it was pleasant; and bowed his shoulder to bear, and became a servant unto forced labor.

49:16-17 Dan shall judge his people, as one of the tribes of Israel. Dan shall be a serpent by the way, an adder in the path that biteth the horse heels, so that his rider shall fall backward.

:18 (Judah) I have waited for thy salvation O, Lord.

:19 Gad, a troop shall overcome him; but he shall overcome at the last.

:20 Out of Asher his bread shall be fat, and he shall yield royal dainties.

:21 Naphtali is a hind let loose; he giveth beautiful words.

:22-26 Joseph is a fruitful bough, even a fruitful bough by a well, whose branches run over the wall. The archers have harassed him, and shot at him and hated him; but his bow abode in strength, and the arms of his hands were made strong by the hands of the mighty God of Jacob (from there is the shepherd, the stone of Israel), Even by the God of thy father, who shall help thee; and by the Almighty, who shall bless thee with blessings of heaven above, blessings of the deep that lieth under, blessings of the breasts, and of the womb. The blessings of thy father have prevailed above the blessings of my progenitors (ancestors) unto the utmost bound of the everlasting hills; they shall be on the head of Joseph, and on the crown of the head of him that was separate from his brethren.

NOTE: Joseph had preeminence over his brothers throughout the remainder of his life.

:27 Benjamin shall consume as a wolf; in the morning he shall devour the prey, and at night he shall divide the spoil.

(Both of the two men in the Bible named Saul were descendants of the tribe of Benjamin.)

49:28-33 All these are the twelve tribes of Israel: and this is that which their father spoke unto them, and blessed them; every one according to his blessing, blessed them. And he charged them, and said unto them, I am to be gathered unto my people: bury me with my fathers in the cave that is in the field of Ephron, the Hittite, In the cave that is in the field of Machpelah, which is before Mamre, in the land of Canaan, which Abraham bought with the field of Ephron, the Hittite, for a possession of a burying place. There they buried Abraham and Sarah, his wife; there they buried Isaac and Rebecca, his wife; and there I buried Leah. The purchase of the field and of the cave that is therein was from the children of Heth. And when Jacob had made an end of commanding his sons, he gathered up his feet into the bed and yielded up the ghost (died), and was gathered unto his people.

Psalm 37:37 Mark the perfect man and behold the upright; for the end of that man is peace.

Genesis
Chapter 50

50:1-2 And Joseph fell upon his father's face, and wept upon him, and kissed him. And Joseph commanded his servants, and the physicians embalmed Israel (Jacob).

God had assured Jacob prior to his entering Egypt: "Joseph shall put his hand upon your eyes." (**Genesis 46:4**) And so it was at the moment of his death.

The embalming process developed by Egyptians has never been the practice of Jews. Even today, deceased Jews are not embalmed. Holes are drilled in the bottom of coffins to allow air to speed up body decomposition. Perhaps Joseph ordered the embalming to ensure Jacob's body would not deteriorate before he could be returned to Canaan's land for burial.

50:3 And forty days were fulfilled for him; for so are fulfilled the days of those who are embalmed: and the Egyptians mourned for him threescore and ten days.

Impressively even the Egyptians mourned for Jacob the customary forty days.

50:4-5 And when the days of his mourning were past, Joseph spoke unto the house of Pharaoh, saying, If now I have found grace in your eyes, speak, I pray you, in the ears of Pharaoh, saying, My father made me swear, saying, Lo, I die: in my grave which I have digged for me in the land of Canaan, there shalt thou bury me. Now therefore let me go up, I pray thee, and bury my father, and I will come again.

Joseph made his request and pledged to return. He was free and, yet, not free. It was actually God who had given his life for a ransom of his people. Had he stayed in the land of Canaan the lives of those in Goshen could have been jeopardized.

50:6-9 And Pharaoh said, Go up, and bury thy father, according as he made thee swear. And Joseph went up to bury his father; and with him went up all of the servants of Pharaoh, the elders of his house, and all the elders of the land of Egypt, and all the house of Joseph, and his brethren, and his father's house: only their little ones, and their flocks, and their herds, they left in the land of Goshen. And there went up with him both chariots and horseman; and it was a very great company.

What a caravan! And it showed that Joseph and his family were greatly honored.

50:10-14 and they came to the threshing floor of Atad, which is beyond Jordan, and there they mourned with a great and very strong lamentation: and he made a mourning for his father seven days. And when the inhabitants of the land, the Canaanites, saw the mourning in the threshing floor of Atad, they said, This is a grievous mourning to the Egyptians: wherefore the name of it was called Abelmizraim (meaning mourning of the Egyptians,) which is beyond the Jordan. And his sons did unto him according as he had commanded them; for his sons carried him into the land of Canaan and buried him in the cave of the field of Machpelah, which Abraham bought with the field for a possession of a burying place of Ephron, the Hittite, before Mamre. And Joseph returned into Egypt, he, and his brethren, and all that went up with him to bury his father, after he had buried his father.

50:15-18 And when Joseph's brethren saw that their father was dead, they said, Joseph will perhaps hate us, and will certainly requite us all the evil which we did unto him. And they sent a messenger unto Joseph, saying, Thy father did command before he died saying, So shall ye say unto Joseph, Forgive, I pray thee now, the trespass of thy brethren, and their sin; for they did unto thee evil: and now, we pray thee, forgive the trespass of thy servants of the God of thy father. And Joseph wept when they spoke unto him. And his brethren also went and fell down before his face; and they said, Behold, we are thy servants.

Seventeen years had passed since Jacob and his sons had come to dwell in Egypt and yet he was still keenly aware of the need of his sons to seek Joseph's forgiveness. Joseph's weeping demonstrated his heart was tender toward them. And, just as his God-given dreams had foretold, his brothers fell down before his face and declared that they were his servants.

50:19-21 And Joseph said unto them, Fear not for am I in the place of God? But as for you, ye thought evil against me; but God meant it unto good, to bring to pass, as it is this day to save many people alive. Now therefore fear ye not; I will nourish you, and your little ones. And he comforted them, and spoke kindly unto them.

Joseph knew that God had a greater purpose beyond his own suffering. He loved God enough to allow great adversity to work together for greater yet unseen good. Perhaps you will allow him to do the same in your life.

Romans 8:28 And we know that all things work together for good to them that love God, to them who are the called according to his purpose.

50:22-26 And Joseph dwelt in Egypt, he, and his father's house: and Joseph lived a hundred and ten years. And Joseph saw Ephraim's children to the third generation: the children also of Machir, the son of Manasseh, were brought up upon Joseph's knees. And Joseph said unto his brethren, I die: and God will surely visit you, and bring you out of this land unto the land which he swore to give to Abraham, to Isaac, and to Jacob. And Joseph took an oath of the children of Israel, saying, God will surely visit you, and ye shall carry up my bones from here. So Joseph died, being a hundred and ten years old: and they embalmed him, and he was put in a coffin in Egypt.

Joseph lived in Egypt ninety-three years though his heart remained in Canaan. He, like his father, wanted to be buried in the land of Canaan along with his forefathers. God did visit them and deliver them from Egypt some 430 years after they arrived there.

According to God's design, (**Exodus 1:8** and **Acts 7:18**,) another king or pharaoh arose, who knew not Joseph.
God's clock was ticking and it was going home time for the people of God.

Exodus 13:19 And Moses took the bones of Joseph with him; for he had solemnly sworn (to) the children of Israel saying, God will surely visit you, and ye shall carry up my bones away from here with you.

Joshua 24:32 And the bones of Joseph, which the children of Israel brought up out of Egypt, buried they in Shechem, in a plot of ground which Jacob bought from the sons of Hamor, the father of Shechem, for an hundred pieces of silver; and it became the inheritance of the children of Joseph.

Here are but a few of the many similarities between Joseph and Jesus:

They both were shepherds, loved by their fathers, hated by their brethren, rejected by their own, and given Gentile brides. They both were thirty years old when their ministries began. They both were betrayed, stripped of their blood-drenched coats, condemned with two other men (one was freed, the other died,) both were sold for the price of a slave.

The numerous comparisons between Joseph and Jesus are fascinating with some being obvious and others hidden. But all are there for our discovery and delight.

PSALM 23 and JOHN 10:1-18

Of the 150 psalms recorded in Jewish and Christian Bibles forty-nine percent (or 73) are accredited to King David. Of those, Psalm Twenty-Three is an all-time favorite; especially comforting, often memorized and frequently quoted. Pastors depend on the 23rd Psalm as an effective antidote for grief-stricken mourners. Its melodious tone is known to resonate reassurance.

Our shepherd-boy king wrote about what his life's experience had taught.

23:1 The Lord is my shepherd; I shall not want.

David knew firsthand of the sacrificial life of a shepherd. He knew what it was to lay down his life to protect his sheep. He was only a youth when he slew a lion and a bear with his hands in order to deliver his lambs. And, because he knew his God, he confidently proclaimed, "The Lord is my shepherd."

23:2 He maketh me to lie down in green pastures; he leadeth me beside still waters.

Sheep are easily frightened. When fearful, an entire herd may stampede off a cliff. They have no weapons; offensive or defensive. Sheep are absolutely dependent upon the care of their shepherd. They know that he will defend them. They know they are safe and protected even though there are many predators.

It is the shepherd who provides the lush green pastures. The word "pastures" is plural because the shepherd provides many pastures. He rotates the herd's grazing to prevent them from devastating the land by eating the very root of the vegetation. If left to themselves, the lambs would ravage the land. You are one of his lambs; don't be surprised when God rotates your pasture.

As the shepherd goes before to open a new gate to allow grazing in a fresh pasture, the older ewes and rams keep their eyes upon him and anticipate what he is about to do. They can be seen running and jumping with joy to enter a fresh pasture. The sheep of the Lord's pasture are truly blessed by his wonderful care.

Psalm 100:3 ... we are his people, and the sheep of his pasture.

Hebrews 13:5 ... be content with such things as ye have; for he hath said, I will never leave nor forsake thee.

Our contentment doesn't consist of the things we possess, but in the faithful loving care of our Shepherd and his promise to never forsake us.

One modern-day shepherd was saddened to see his neighbor's sheep pressing against a fence that divided their properties. His lambs were lean, deprived of care, and burdened with parasites. They longed to be free, but their shepherd did not care for them. In contrast, lambs who belong to Jesus are always well cared for.

Another distinguishing trait of sheep is that they must be led; therefore, the shepherd goes before them, and they follow. Other herds; such as cattle, horses, and buffalo must be driven. Sheep have no leader among their own.

If you are being driven, look behind you to see who the driver is; it is not the Lord. Our Shepherd gently leads. He has the path mapped out, and he alone knows where he is leading his lambs. Sheep may panic if someone attempts to drive them. They must follow the leading of their own gentle shepherd.

Sheep are not known for intelligence. Undiscerning lambs will stop and drink out of any stream although it may be polluted with parasites and disease-causing bacteria.

One of the benefits of salvation written about by King David in Psalm 103 is that Jesus has healed all our disease. Think of the word "disease" as "dis-ease." Our Good Shepherd has healed everything that would cause us to be "dis-eased." We are quieted and not disquieted. We are comforted and not discomforted.

Sheep are fearful and will not lie down in exposed pastures unless the shepherd is there to guard. Without anyway of defending themselves from predators, lambs rely entirely on their shepherd.

The shepherd has gone before, and he knows how to lead his own to clear streams of fresh flowing water and to wells of refreshing pure water. How blessed are his lambs!

Sheep imitate behaviors just as people do. Sometimes behavior fads can even sweep through congregations captivating and ensnaring unperceptive members. These fads usually don't last long but can have a lasting effect on those mesmerized by them.

A shepherd told of going out to his barn early one morning to open the gate for his lambs. He playfully stuck his staff over the gate opening. To his surprise, the first lamb leaped right over it. The shepherd laughed and put his staff down, but to his utter amazement each of the remaining herd stopped at the spot where the first lamb leaped, and each one leaped too. It was a clear case of "monkey see, monkey do." Followers of Jesus do not need to mimic behaviors of other lambs; they need only to follow Jesus and do as he does.

My daughter and I visited a church she was considering attending. Arriving just as the service began, we sat in the back of the filled sanctuary. What we witnessed, as the worship progressed would have been comical had it not been so sad. Our vantage spot provided a panoramic view of the congregation. Men across the sanctuary began jumping in place with their hands straight by their sides like they were on pogo sticks. Were they inspired by God or merely giving a programmed response? In a short time, we saw that a dozen or so men had joined in. And we wondered.

23:3 He restoreth my soul; he leadeth me in paths of righteousness for his name's sake

The shepherd offers "redemptive chastisement" to rebellious lambs. You may have seen a picture or a statue of a shepherd carrying a lamb on his shoulders. He may be carrying a rebellious lamb back to safety within his fold after having rescued it from a crevasse, a cliff, or whatever dangerous situation its rebellion had gotten it into. He has rescued this lamb many times. The lamb will not obey his voice. He then simply breaks the lamb's leg and places it upon his shoulders. It is no longer able to run away. He then carries the lamb until it is completely healed.

During the time of healing, the shepherd strokes the lamb, talks and sings to it, and it learns to eat out of his hand. By the time its leg is healed, it loves the care of the shepherd and won't leave his side. The lamb has come to trust the shepherd and is now content to walk alongside him. Isn't it just like Jesus to carry us until we are completely healed? Some pictures show a shepherd who can hardly walk because of his lambs crowding around. Is it any wonder that those who depend on Jesus, love him so and walk close beside him?

> **Isaiah 53: 6** All we like sheep have gone astray; we have turned everyone to his own way ...

> **1st Peter 2:25** For ye were as sheep going astray, but are now returned unto the Shepherd and Bishop of our souls.

122

The Bible speaks of only one man named David. During a time of his life, he was a rebellious lamb. Drawing from his background as a shepherd-boy, King David wrote a beautiful psalm in which he poured out his heart to God after the prophet Nathan exposed his great sin.

Psalm 51:8 Make me to hear joy and gladness that <u>the bones which thou hast broken may rejoice</u>.

As a shepherd, he understood the dealings of God with his own. Writing as an allegory, he acknowledged that he knew who had figuratively broken his bones, and he understood why.

According to **Exodus 12:46** and **Numbers 9:12** a sacrificial lamb was not to have any bone broken. It is important for us to understand why Jesus, the Lamb of God, did not have any bone broken. The two others crucified with Jesus were malefactors (G#2557 criminal, evil-doer), and, as such, had their legs broken. The Lamb of God, Jesus, was **not** a rebellious lamb.

Hebrews 12:2 tells us that he despised the shame of the cross but that he endured because of the joy that was set before him.

His Bride is the joy set before him! Lord, grant that we walk worthily during our lifetimes.

If a sheep continued in rebellion after repeated rescues and attempts at correction had failed, and especially if it began leading other sheep astray, the shepherd would take his knife and slaughter the lamb by slicing its throat.

Sheep, like some people, are noted for causing injury to one another by backbiting. Backbiters come from the rear and chomp hard on their victim before vanishing into the herd. Their victim may not see who the backbiter is but only feel the pain. Be assured, dear one, our all-seeing Good Shepherd knows.

Whenever you are injured or in need of restoration, remember what King David said, "He restoreth my soul."

When left to themselves, the paths of lambs become deep ruts and trenches as their wool is entangled with mud and debris adding to their misery. If your path entangles you with misery, check to make sure you are on the path he has chosen.

> **Proverbs 3:17** (speaking of God's wisdom) Her ways are ways of pleasantness, and all her paths are peace.

The shepherd knows when winter is coming. There will be hungry vicious predators waiting to devour his precious lambs. He knows the foliage will be covered with ice and snow. There will be no provision made unless they move on. Parts of the way are steep and treacherous. The lambs must follow the shepherd while keeping their eyes and ears fixed on him. The way is hard. The way is difficult. The shepherd moves slowly because the younger lambs have not passed this way before. Some would rather turn back than to continue through a blinding blizzard with only the voice of their shepherd to guide. Their safety and well-being depends on his care and on their obedience.

You may have lost a child, grandchild, or other loved-one. Picture the all-knowing shepherd standing by the side of a stream. The ewe is there and is not willing to ford the stream. Forcing her may cause her to panic and that may very well cost her life. So the shepherd gently lifts her young lamb into his bosom and walks to the other side. He knows the mother ewe will quickly follow because she wants to be with her little lamb.

> **23:4** Yea, though I walk through the valley of
> the shadow of death, I will fear no evil; for thou
> art with me; thy rod and thy staff they comfort me.

When we leave this world, we pass through the valley of the shadow of death but without actually facing death; meaning separation from God. The Lamb of God has done that for us. He has conquered and destroyed death for us.

Psychologists know one of the primary fears of children is that of being abandoned. Our Shepherd is Emanuel (God with us). In **John 14:16**, Jesus promised that his Spirit would abide with us forever as a comforter.

The shepherd's rod became a symbol of authority after the exodus when Moses used his rod to bring hail, lightning, locusts, and to part the Red Sea. The rod then became a scepter used by kings to symbolize authority.

The rod also represents comfort to the sheep in that it is used to examine them. One by one, in the cool of the evening, they come to pass under the rod. The shepherd uses his rod to part their wool. Wool in scripture may at times represent pride. When his rod parts the wool, the shepherd can easily remove what they are powerless to remove themselves. They cannot see what is causing them trouble, grief, and pain. There can be thorns, thistles, or ticks and other parasites. The lambs delight in being examined knowing they cannot relieve their own suffering. As you walk with Jesus, you may often pass under his rod. Allow him to examine your innermost heart and to remove all that is detrimental to your well-being.

The staff is used to rescue lambs caught in crevasses. And it is used to right a sheep that has become cast; that is "down and not able to get up." After grazing for a long time, they may lie down, but then their stomachs swell with gases. Their legs are so short that they cannot get up again. In this vulnerable position, they are easy prey for predators. Their anxious cry can quickly bring a hungry lion. The shepherd must remain alert to the distressed cry of a cast lamb. The shepherd will risk his own life to save his lambs.

Psalm 37:23-24 (written by King David) The steps of a good man are ordered by the Lord, and he delighteth in his way. Though he fall, he shall not be utterly <u>cast down</u>; for the Lord upholdeth him with his hand.

The staff is also used to touch a favorite lamb that walks close to the shepherd. It looks as though they are walking hand in hand. Image the little lamb scampering alongside with his head held high sort of prancing as he goes. What a delightful scene. And how content is this little lamb to be walking alongside his protector and provider.

23:5 Thou preparest a table before me in the presence of mine enemies; thou anointest my head with oil; my cup runneth over.

Here again is the shepherd going on before to make ready. This verse refers to the "tableland" (plateau or flat surface) prepared in advance by the shepherd for his lambs. He has anticipated the needs of his own and has already removed the delicious bright red berries that his lambs wouldn't distinguish as poisonous. As part of his preparation, he has removed all torn hedges and briars.

The shepherd anoints the lamb's entire head with oil. It goes over its ears, eyes, nose, and mouth areas preventing flies and other insects from tormenting. Lambs are even defenseless against these tiny insects until the anointing oil covers. Sheep of uncaring shepherds have been seen bashing their heads against rocks in a vain effort to be relieved of their tormentors.

This reminds me of people who seek medical help when deliverance from evil spirits is what is needed. The oil symbolizes the outpouring of the Holy Spirit, and the tormentors, the harassment of evil spirits. Keep in mind that the anointing (or the outpouring) of the Holy Spirit only comes from being in his presence. We must long to live in the Lord's presence.

Living in his presence means our cups run over with joy and gladness, so there is plenty of overflow for others.

> **23:6** Surely goodness and mercy shall follow me all the days of my life; and I will dwell in the house of the Lord forever.

As we are following Jesus, goodness and mercy are following us. All of his paths are righteousness, mercy, and truth not only for today's path but all the days of our lives.

King David began and ended this psalm by declaring the Lord. He had learned what it was to be a shepherd. He also learned what it was to be a lamb whose leg had to be broken. And he trusted that he would dwell in the house of the Lord forever.

I recommend reading, "Reflections from the Flock" by Ken Johnson and Robert Tamasy and "A Shepherd Looks At Psalm 23" by Phillip Keller for additional insight into the relationship between a shepherd and his sheep.

Let us go on to John 10:1-18 where Jesus revealed himself as the Good Shepherd.

John 10:1-18

Each of the sixty-six books of the Bible contain words that make it distinctive. The Gospel of John is always a favorite. Twenty-five scriptures record Jesus using the term, "Verily, verily," and ALL of these are recorded in the Gospel of John. The word "sent" is prevalent in the Gospel of John where it is used fifty-six times. If you were asked which of the four gospels tells the story of Jesus instructing a man to, "Go, wash in the pool of Siloam (which is by interpretation, Sent)," you would know immediately that it is recorded in the Gospel of John.

Only in John's gospel are the seven "I AM" declarations made by Jesus recorded.

6:35   I am the bread of life.
8:12   I am the light.
11:25 I am the resurrection and the life.
14:6   I am the way, the truth, and the life.
15:1,5 I am the true wine

The two other "I AM" declarations occur in **John 10** where we find him teaching a parable to the Pharisees.

129

10:1 Verily, verily, I say unto you, He that entereth not by the door into the sheepfold, but climbeth up some other way, the same is a thief and a robber.

The ancient public sheepfold is still in use today by shepherds who bring their sheep there for safekeeping during the night. The sheepfold in this story represents the nation of Israel. Jesus began by saying that he who entered in not by the door is a thief and a robber, and later he will declare that he is the door.

10:2-3 But he that entereth in by the door is the shepherd of the sheep. To him the porter openeth, and the sheep hear his voice, and he calleth his own by name, and leadeth them out.

Jesus let them know that he came by way of the door (the Spirit) and that he came in legally. Shepherds come to the door or entrance in the morning and call to the porter to open the door. The porter represents the Holy Spirit; he is the keeper; the protector of the sheepfold. He knows the voices of the shepherds and opens the door to allow the sheep to respond to their shepherd's voice. Jesus was manifested to call his sheep (that's us) out of the common or public sheepfold unto himself. He calls today to "whosoever will" to come and follow him.

Sheep wear no visible mark of ownership. They are never branded. They are known only by their responses to the shepherd's voice. If you are one of his, you don't need to wear a visible mark or brand.

A pastor told of touring in Jerusalem and of seeing two shepherds with their flocks on a hillside. He watched as they called to one another. He continued to observe and was astonished as they began walking toward each other. He thought, "Oh, what a mess. They'll never get their flocks untangled." He continued to gaze as the shepherds briefly visited and then parted. He was amazed to see that each lamb followed his own shepherd. The shepherds called out their own by name, and their own quickly followed.

Have you ever wondered about people who hear the true word of God and who fail to respond? Or about those who walk in his light for a while and then depart into error and gross darkness? Do they not hear the Shepherd or do they not heed his voice?

10:4-5 And when he putteth forth his own sheep, he goeth before them, and the sheep follow him; for they know his voice. And a stranger they will not follow, but will flee from him; for they know not the voice of strangers.

Years ago I read a story in *Reader's Digest* written by a hospital nurse telling how one patient responded to her checking the intercom system in his room. She called out, "Johnny, if you can hear me, let me know." When he failed to respond, she said, "Johnny, I know you're in there. Please speak to me." And little Johnny, in fearless childlike boldness, asked, "What do you want wall?"

Shouldn't we, as Christians, at least check out the voice giving us instructions?

3rd John :4 I have no greater joy than to hear my children walk in truth.

Make it your life's goal to bring joy to your Father by walking in his truth. Our very lives, as well as our eternal destinies, depend on rightly discerning what voice we are hearing and heeding.

1st John 4:1 Beloved, believe not every spirit, but try the spirits whether they are of God.

Bopping through life from one blunder to another can be avoided by those who "try the spirits."

The beginning words of the Book of Isaiah contain some of the saddest words found in scripture.

Isaiah 1:2-3 Hear, O heavens, and give ear, O earth; for the Lord hath spoken; I have nourished and brought up children, and they have rebelled against me. The ox knoweth his owner, and the ass, his master's crib, but Israel doth not know, my people doth not consider.

An even sadder truth is that there are many within the sheepfold (the visible church of today) who do not know his voice and who do not consider him.

John 10:6 This parable spoke Jesus unto them; but they understood not what things they were which he spoke unto them.

Jesus was speaking to Pharisees who were infuriated because he had healed a man who had been born blind. (**John 9:1**)

He told them that because they were spiritually blind their sin would remain. Interestingly, the Pharisees were still debating this nitpicking matter-that-didn't-matter all the way to 10:21. That's sixty-two verses! It's typical of the religious-without-relationship crowd to focus on what doesn't matter. Jesus told the scribes and Pharisees that they were hypocrites and added, "Ye blind guides, who strain at a gnat and swallow a camel." (**Matthew 23:24**)

In fact, all of ninth chapter of John is devoted to the unnamed formerly-blind man, to the spiritually-blind Pharisees, and to Jesus' reply to both. This is mentioned because it is apparent that Jesus was <u>demonstrating</u> who he was before he was to <u>declare</u> who he was.

John 9:34 states that the formerly-blind man was "cast out" of the synagogue by the Pharisees.

The next verse is of special interest.
John 10:7 Jesus heard that they had cast him out; <u>and when he had found him</u>, He said unto him, 'Dost thou believe on the Son of God?

We are well aware of scriptures telling how people crowded around as they tried to get closer to Jesus. But here we find Jesus demonstrating what he would later declared in **10:11,14**, "I am the good shepherd." The good shepherd searches for his lambs, right?

10:7-8 Then said Jesus unto them, Verily, verily, I say unto you, I am the door of the sheep. All that ever came before me are thieves and robbers; but the sheep did not hear them.

Here Jesus gave his second "Verily, verily" within the same discourse which is a clue for us to understand that these are important scriptures. The third chapter of John records Jesus speaking three "Verily, verily" statements to Nicodemus. And we all appreciate and know that discourse is especially important.

An example of those who had gone before him declaring that they were "the way" is found in **Acts 5:34-39** where we find Gamaliel reminding the seventy member Sanhedrin of Thèudas and of Judas of Galilee who each drew away many people unto themselves but who both proved to be false.

Verses 9-11 contain two of his seven "I AM" declarations.

John 10:9-11 I am the door; by me if any man enter in, he shall be saved, and shall go in and out, and find pasture. The thief cometh not but to steal, and to kill, and to destroy; I am come that they might have life, and that they might have it more abundantly. I am the good shepherd; for the good shepherd giveth his life for the sheep.

10:12-14 But he that is a hireling, and not the shepherd, whose own the sheep are not, seeth the wolf coming, and leaveth the sheep, and fleeth; and the wolf catcheth them, and scattereth the sheep. The hireling fleeth, because he is a hireling, and careth not for the sheep. <u>I am the good shepherd</u> and know my sheep, and am known of mine.

This was the third time, in addressing the people that he said his sheep know him. People can argue over scriptures and dispute differences in doctrine, but what matters most is whether or not you know his voice and are following him. The Pharisees with all their "vain traditions of men" did not know God. They only had "a form of godliness" (or outward show).

10:15-16 As the Father knoweth me, even so know I the Father; and I lay down my life for the sheep. And other sheep I have, that are not of this fold; them also I must bring, and <u>they shall hear my voice</u>; and there shall be one fold, and one shepherd.

The "other sheep" are the Gentiles who are then called to hear his voice. Remember what the Apostle Paul, who was a Pharisee and son of a Pharisee, said after the Jews in Rome rejected his message.

Acts 28:28 Be it known, therefore, unto you that the salvation of God is sent unto the Gentiles, and that <u>they will hear it</u>.

10:17-18 Therefore doth my Father love me, because I lay down my life that I might take it again. No man taketh it from me, but I lay it down of myself. I have power to lay it down, and I have power to take it again. This commandment have I received of my Father.

What is this commandment of the Father?
Hebrews 9:22 states, "... without shedding of blood is no remission (of sin).

Leviticus 17:11 For the life of the flesh is in the blood ... for it is the blood that maketh an atonement for the soul.

As he prepared to sacrifice Isaac, Abraham told his son: **Genesis 22:8** My son, God will provide himself a lamb ...

And he did, didn't he?

Genesis 4:4 Abel offered a lamb for his own sin.
Exodus 12:3 The blood of a spotless lamb was offered for the sin of each household.
Leviticus 16:29-34, 23:26-32 A lamb was offered for the sin of the nation.
John 1:29 When John looked up and saw Jesus, he said, "Behold, the Lamb of God that taketh away the sin of the world."

Blessed be the Lamb of God

BOOK OF RUTH

The Book of Ruth is a true love story; a story of redemption. It's the story of two unlikely people who meet in an unlikely circumstance arranged by God. Neither could have guessed that their union would produce the godly seed the Lord desired. Boaz could not have known that his name and the names of both his wife and his mother (Rahab) would be listed in Messiah's genealogy. (Matthew 1:5) God had determined to bless this couple with a true love as he fulfilled his purpose.

Ruth was from the country of Moab which no longer exists. That land is now a part of Jordan. Moses died upon Mt. Nebo in Moab. God twice referred to Moab as his washpot. (Psalm 60:8, 108:9)

The Book of Ruth is one of two named for women; the other the Book of Esther. The Book of Ruth is the only Bible account of a kinsman redeemer. Although only consisting of four chapters, it gives a full rich picture of the Lord Jesus Christ, our Blessed Redeemer and his Gentile Bride.

The word "redemption" is used in the original King James New Testament rather than "atonement," because atonement only covers sin; whereas redemption means a full price had been paid. Those who are redeemed are entirely free.

The events recorded in the Book of Ruth do not include the wars and bloodshed typical of many Old Testament books. Curiously, prayer is not mentioned just as God is not mentioned in the ten chapters of the Book of Esther. However, both books record many providential events orchestrated by God. His presence is woven throughout the tapestry of both books.

Of the thirty-nine Old Testament books, the Book of Ruth is one of eleven whose author is unknown. We owe a great deal to these unknown authors who are only known to God.

It is hoped that this study will enrich your heart as God discloses some of his mysterious ways of accomplishing his purposes in the lives of individuals who are unaware that they are an important part of his eternal plan; just as you are.

Ruth
Chapter 1

1:1 Now it came to pass in the days when the judges ruled, that there was a famine in the land. And a certain man of Bethlehem-Judah went to sojourn in the country of Moab, he, and his wife, and his two sons.

Scripture tells that God used famine thirteen times as a judgment. This was one of those judgments. The time of the judges was a time of deplorable moral and spiritual apostasy. The time that the judges ruled were dark days and these were the darkest of the dark. The phrase "when the judges ruled" brings to mind the time we live in when our nation's highest court, the U.S. Supreme Court, rules supreme while denying the Supreme Ruler, the Lord Jesus Christ. The judgments of these appointed rulers have catapulted our nation into the darkest of dark days.

Bethlehem means "house of bread;" whereas Judah means "praise." Twice in Psalms written by King David (60:8 and 108:9) God is quoted as having said, "Moab is my washpot." Elimelech left the house of bread and praise and journeyed with his family to dwell in God's washpot. The people of Moab were the descendants of the incestuous union of Lot and his first-born daughter.

1:2-4 And the name of the man was Elimelech, and the name of his wife, Naomi, and the name of his two sons, Mahlon and Chilion, Ephrathites of Bethlehem-

139

Judah. And they came into the country of Moab, and continued there. And Elimelech, Naomi's husband died; and she was left, and her two sons. And they took themselves wives of the women of Moab; the name of the one was Orpah, and the name of the other, Ruth; and they dwelt there about ten years.

Orpah means, "deer or fawn," which is a graceful and pretty animal but is easily frightened and not easily tamed. Ruth means "friend or companion." Aside from Jesus, throughout the Bible few friends can be found as faithful as this young damsel Ruth.

1:5 And Mahlon and Chilion died also, both of them; and the woman was left (bereaved) of her sons and her husband.

Mahlon means "sick" and Chilion means "pining." Choosing their sons' names may have been an indication of their parents' dire expectation.

Mahlon and Chilion married Moabites knowing that Mosaic Law forbids marrying foreign women. However, we will learn that God had a plan; a wonderful plan.

According to God's providence, neither Orpah nor Ruth bore a child during these marriages of "about ten years." Had either woman produced an offspring, the plan of God may have been averted.

1:6 Then she arose with her daughters-in-law, that she might return from the country of Moab; for she had

140

heard in the country of Moab how the Lord had visited his people in giving them bread.

This welcomed news arrived right on time. Naomi's life was being directed by the Blessed Controller without her awareness. Though only aware of her own loss and misery, this prodigal's heart was stirred to return to her homeland.

1:7-10 Wherefore, she went out of the place where she was, and her two daughters-in-law with her; and they went on the way to return unto the land of Judah. And Naomi said unto her two daughters-in-law, Go, return each to her mother's house; the Lord deal kindly with you, as you have dealt with the dead, and with me. The Lord grant you that ye may find rest, each of you in the house of her husband. Then she kissed them; and they lifted up their voice, and wept. And they said unto her, Surely we will return with thee unto thy people.

Both daughters followed Naomi expecting to journey alongside her. Each daughter-in-law pledged to go with Naomi and to be with her people. But Ruth wanted something more; she wanted the God of Israel to be her God. Many pledge to follow Jesus all the way to the glory world, but not everyone completes the journey. This young damsel was to complete her journey.

1:11-14 And Naomi said, Turn again, my daughters. Why will ye go with me? Are there yet any more sons in my womb, that they may be your husbands? Turn again, my daughters, go your way; for I am too old to have a husband. If I should say, I have hope; if I should have a husband also tonight, and should bear also sons, would ye tarry till they were grown? Would ye refrain from marrying? Nay, my daughters; for it grieveth me much for your sakes that the hand of the Lord has gone out against me. And they lifted up their voice, and wept again; and Orpah kissed her mother-in-law, **but** Ruth clung to her.

Naomi called Orpah and Ruth "my daughters" three times signifying that their relationship was not severed by the deaths of her husband and sons. I imagine that few Israelite women would have embraced foreign daughters-in-law. Naomi stated that it "grieveth her much for your sakes that the hand of the Lord has gone out against me." She blamed God for having "gone out against her." Her reasoning may have been typical for some who suffer grief, hopelessness, and helplessness. She blamed God for her circumstance much like Adam blamed God when he said, "The woman whom thou gavest to be with me ..."

Naomi really laid it on the line not promising them anything or guaranteeing a life of prosperity. These women were heathen Moabite widows, and were without sons. Choosing to follow Naomi to a land and a people unknown to them would be quite a choice.

Following Jesus involves weeping along the way as decisions are made that set the course for future events in our lives. Note that both women wept when their mother-in-law encouraged them to turn back.

We are told in **Hebrews 10:38**, "... but if any man draw back, my soul shall have no pleasure in him."

Naomi kissed both Orpah and Ruth signifying her love and acceptance of them. As the story unfolds, we will see that Orpah may have produced a righteous seed, but, when given a choice, she choose to return to the place of known security and "little g" gods".

Each of these three women were at a pivotal point in her life. It must have been quite a sight; the three weeping women huddled in their customary garb. But not all their tears come from a circumcised heart. Ruth's heart had been circumcised and she knew it. God had brought them to a crossroad and left the choice to them, as he does with us.

Joshua encouraged the Israelites with these words found in:

Joshua 24:14-15 Now, therefore, fear the Lord, and serve him in sincerity and in truth; and put away the gods which your fathers served on the other side of the river, and in Egypt, and serve ye the Lord. And if it seem evil unto you to serve the Lord, choose you this day whom ye will serve, whether the gods which your fathers served that were on the other side of the river, or the gods of the Amorites, in whose land ye dwell; but as for me and my house, we will serve the Lord.

Undoubtedly, as you walk with the Lord, you will come to many crossroads that require a decision. Some may be quite unexpected, and you may have to make decisions without clear guidance from the Lord.

143

I was at a perplexing crossroad many decades ago when he left the choice of which road to take to me. I have never regretted taking his hand and launching out into life's greatest adventure; walking with Jesus! Remember, those who walk with him always reach their destination.

1:15-17 And she said, Behold, thy sister-in-law is gone back unto her people, and unto her gods; return thou after thy sister-in-law. And Ruth said, Entreat me not to leave thee, or to return (turn away) from following thee; for where thou goest, I will go; and where thou lodgest, I will lodge: thy people shall be my people, and thy God, my God. Where thou diest, will I die, and there will I be buried; the Lord do so to me, and more also, if anything but death part thee and me.

Orpah departed without fanfare and, thus, waltzed off the pages of life to return to her heathen people and to her "little g gods" never to be heard from again.

Naomi didn't express grief over Orpah's choice of returning to her people and to her "little g gods", instead, she encouraged Ruth to do the same. Ruth's heart, as well as her destiny, had already been set. Naomi may have been testing Ruth's decision.

Ruth, precious Ruth, eloquently and irrevocably spoke the determination of her heart. God had chosen her for a special assignment, and she embraced it without knowing what it was or where it would lead. She was in it to stay; even to the grave. Some may think that young

144

people make wrong choices. Ruth is referred to as young damsel five times in these four chapters, and every decision she made was what God desired. (I wish I could say the same about my own choices.) This young damsel thought that she would be a childless poor widow and expected nothing more than continued hardship.

The very words spoken by Ruth three-thousand years ago are still regarded as the most sincere statement of love and devotion. Her words are oftentimes recited as part of wedding vows even today. You can rest assured that Ruth never dreamed of such a thing! God has ways of honoring those who honor him, my friend.

And, best of all, she knew that Naomi's God was her God. This is truly remarkable when we consider that Ruth saw the bitterness in Naomi's heart toward the Lord. What matters to you and to me is what is in our own hearts.

1:18 When she saw that she was steadfastly determined to go with her, then she ceased speaking unto her.

The enemy of your soul will cease speaking when he sees you have uncovered his lies. True enough, he will bring other tormenting thoughts; but rest assured, God will strengthen you as you see them for what they are.

James 1:8 A double-minded man is unstable in all his ways.

Those with a double-mind will have a half-hearted commitment and will be tormented for sure. While those who abide in his presence are kept in the wonderful peace that passes understanding.

1:19-21 So they two went until they came to Bethlehem. And it came to pass, when they were come to Bethlehem, that all the city was moved about them, and they said, "Is this Naomi? And she said unto them, Call me not Naomi, call me Mara (bitter) for the Almighty hath dealt very bitterly with me. I went out full, and the Lord hath brought me home again empty. Why, then, call ye me Naomi, seeing the Lord hath testified against me, and the Almighty hath afflicted me?

Wow! This woman didn't mince words when spewing words from her bitter heart. The new name "Mara" that she chose for herself literally means bitter, and it suited her just fine. Her family and acquaintances could hardly believe their eyes when they saw her. This woman with the bitter heart was now care-worn and aged. What is in a person's heart will show on their countenance.

She hurled four accusations against God: the Almighty hath dealt <u>very bitterly</u> with me, the Lord brought me home again empty, the Lord hath testified against me, the Almighty hath afflicted me. This poor woman was so bitter toward the Lord that she couldn't see the greatest blessing standing right by her side: **Ruth!** That's the way it is; when we are bitter, we can't see the blessing. Blaming God will not remedy a heartache but praising him will. Throughout the entire story, no words of gratitude are recorded as having been spoken by Naomi; only her words of bitterness. It is noteworthy that,

146

though Ruth loved Naomi, her mother-in-law's bitterness did not contaminate her. The simple truth was that Ruth had come to love and trust the Lord God of Israel. Letting bitterness have the reigns is a choice just as allowing the Spirit of God to rule our hearts is a choice.

1:22 So Naomi returned, and Ruth the Moabitess, her daughter-in-law, with her, who returned out of the land of Moab; and they came to Bethlehem in the beginning of barley season.

Naomi returned without her husband and sons facing even greater adversity than what they had fled. An older widow with no sons had little hope of a satisfying life.

Naomi expected a dismal future in the town where Jesus was destined to be born. Providentially, they arrived at the beginning of the harvest. It was the appointed time to return home.

Ruth
Chapter 2

2:1 And Naomi had a kinsman of her husband's, a mighty man of wealth, of the family of Elimelech; and his name was Boaz.

Boaz is the other central person of this magnificent love story. His name means "strength," and we will learn that every aspect of his character was marked by strength and integrity. God had made him a mighty man of wealth to enable him to perform his appointed purposes. As the son of the heathen harlot Rahab, he knew firsthand the power of God to transform lives. Note that God graciously honored Rahab by listing her name in the begets as well as in the well-known "faith roll" listed in Hebrews 11:31. What an honor!

2:2 And Ruth, the Moabitess, said unto Naomi, Let me go to the field, and glean ears of corn after him in whose sight I shall find grace. And she said to her, Go, my daughter.

Ruth already had that quiet peace that comes from trusting the Lord. She knew she would find the grace (favor) she needed from the owner of the field but she didn't yet know the owner of the field. She had not come to Bethlehem to beg or be a burden. She came expecting to work to support herself and to provide for her mother-in-law. Gleaning was Ruth's idea, and she sough t Naomi's approval before doing so. She wasn't doing her own thing. She was not ashamed to work this menial task.

Naomi's age and health may have prevented her from offering to help glean or help beat out that which was gleaned. Throughout this four chapter romance, I am struck by Naomi's lack of gratitude though. She would have really been in a fix without the Lord directing the actions of Ruth to her benefit.

In Mosaic Law, God's way of providing for strangers and the poor **(Leviticus 19:9, 23:22 Deuteronomy 24:19)** was to allow them to "glean" from the fields of the wealthy. The gleaners would go behind the harvesters and freely pick the broken and crushed fruit or vegetables that had fallen to the ground. Ruth would not have had understanding of this law had it not been told to her. Perhaps she had seen people gleaning and had inquired about it.

2:3 And she went, and came, and gleaned in the field after the reapers; and her hap was to light on a part of the field belonging unto Boaz, who was of the kindred of Elimelech.

The purposes of God depended upon her being in the right field and at the right time. Providentially, she stopped at the exact spot the Lord God Almighty desired. You'll find the same thing true in your own journey through this pilgrim land.

Some translations today say "she happened to come to a portion of a field belonging to Boaz," rather than "her hap was to light on a part of a field belonging unto

Boaz." God arranged that she just happened upon the right field at the right time. (Smile)

In man's eyes she was a poor stranger gleaning among strangers in the heat of the day struggling to maintain a living with no expectation other than endless days of poverty and hard work.

Ruth will shortly see the providential hand of God move on her behalf. We, like Ruth, make decisions that determine our futures without our being aware. Seeing the hand of the Lord move on our behalf is a thrilling experience that strengthens our relationship with him. The rewards of walking hand in hand with the Lord through much adversity far out-weigh the difficulty.

2:4 And, behold, Boaz came from Bethlehem, and said unto the reapers, The Lord be with you. And they answered him, The Lord bless thee.

This gracious greeting of a wealthy man showed his regard for the Lord and for his reapers, too. And their response signified their respect.

2:5 Then said Boaz unto his servant who was set over the reapers, Whose damsel is this?

This is the part of our story where God's kaleidoscope begins to quickly change the picture. Boaz took notice of the damsel (Hebrew #5291 young woman.) By asking, "Whose damsel is this?" he inquired as to whether or not she was married. Without trying she had caught his eye, and it won't be long until she had his heart!

2:6-7 And the servant who was set over the reapers answered and said, It is the Moabitish damsel who came back with Naomi out of the country of Moab: And she said, I pray you, let me glean and gather after the reapers among the sheaves. So she came, and hath continued even from the morning until now, except that she tarried a little in the house.

This observant overseer gave his observant boss a detailed report of Ruth. And what he reported was music to his ears.

She had asked permission to glean and had only sought rest for a short time in the house. Learning that she was Naomi's daughter-in-law, Boaz understood that she was also a widow.

2:8-9 Then said Boaz unto Ruth, Hearest thou not, my daughter? Go not to glean in another field, neither go from here, but abide here close by my maidens; Let thine eyes be on the field that they do reap, and go thou after them. Have I not charged the young men that they shall not touch thee? And when thou art thirsty, go unto the vessels, and drink of that which the young men have drawn.

When the Lord gives favor, he gives favor! Boaz had already flipped over the young widow from Moab. He assured her that she could be at ease and focus on her gleaning without worrying about being taken advantage of by the young men working the field.

This is the first of four times the term "young men" is used to paint a picture of the situation faced by the young damsel. Boaz invited her to abide in his field alone meaning there would be an abundant supply to meet her needs without her looking elsewhere. Likewise, when we abide with Jesus in his field, he abundantly supplies all our needs so we don't need to look elsewhere.

Ruth did nothing to call attention to herself, did not seek recognition, or reward. We, too, don't need to go out of our way to be noticed when we are walking the path he has mapped out. God alone knows what he is desiring to accomplish in each life.

2:10 Then she fell on her face, and bowed herself to the ground, and said unto him, Why have I found grace in thine eyes, that thou shouldest take knowledge of me, seeing I am a stranger?

Ruth identified herself as a stranger; not as a new convert. She was not delusional concerning her status. She was absolutely amazed and stunned at the favor Boaz extended. When she left her mother-in-law that morning, she had no idea how her mission would turn out. It must have taken a lot of courage to go forth as a stranger in a strange land.

Many a young maiden in Bethlehem-Judah would have been honored to be noticed by this eligible bachelor.

2:11-12 And Boaz answered and said unto her, It hath fully been shown me, all that thou hast done for thy mother-in-law since the death of thine husband, and

152

how thou hast left thy father and thy mother, and the land of thy nativity, and art come unto a people which thou knewest not therefore. The Lord recompense thy work, and a full reward be given thee of the Lord God of Israel, under whose wings thou art come to trust.

God was careful to assure Boaz of Ruth's work ethics and morals. From his statement in verse 11, it's clear he had made a background check on Ruth and that he was impressed by what he had learned. He knew he was enthralled with her when he first saw her and now he was confident he could trust her heart. He acknowledged that Ruth's love and loyalty to her mother-in-law had cost her dearly thus proving his sensitivity to her. And, best of all, he acknowledged that she had come to know the one true God and trusted in him. It is obvious from the blessing he bestowed that he had more than a passing interest. And to think that she must not have looked like a prom date after working in the field since early in the day. This wasn't an ideal setting where the guy meets the girl. It was Ruth's DNA of love and integrity that had made her quite attractive to this wealthy near-kinsman. And, best of all, Boaz knew that, even though her upbringing was thoroughly heathen, her trust in the Lord God of Israel was thoroughly genuine. He knew conversions were real. He also knew his own mother, the harlot Rahab, had been converted to trust in the Lord God Jehovah.

1st Corinthians 4:5 Therefore, judge nothing before the time, until the Lord come, who both will bring to light the hidden things of darkness, and will make manifest the counsels of the hearts; and then shall every man have praise of God.

It may be difficult to imagine God praising you, but be assured that he sees your heart and appreciates your love and devotion. Like Ruth, you will receive a sure reward for your labor of love.

Psalms 126:5-6 They that sow in tears shall reap in joy. He that goeth forth and weepeth, bearing precious seed, shall doubtless come again with rejoicing bringing his sheaves with him.

Now back to our study of Ruth:
Ruth 2:13 Then she said, Let me find favor in thy sight, my lord; for that thou hast comforted me, and because thou hast spoken friendly unto thine handmaid, though I be not like unto one of thine handmaidens.

Ruth further exhibited true humility by expressing her wonderment at his gracious concern although she was not of his people. She could readily agree with **Proverbs 19:12** which states, "The king's favor is like dew upon the grass." Ruth was not accustomed to finding favor; only hardship. Little did she know that she wouldn't be a stranger much longer and before long Boaz would give her more than accolades; he would give her his name!

2:14 And Boaz said unto her, At mealtime come thou hither, and eat of the bread, and dip thy morsel in the vinegar. And she sat beside the reapers; and he reached her parched corn, and she did eat, and was satisfied, and left.

Boaz was very much taken by this woman and went out of his way to see that her needs were met. Once she had eaten, she returned to the field. She didn't lag behind to flirt with this wealthy interested available bachelor. She returned to her commitment to provide for Naomi and herself.

2:15-16 And when she was risen up to glean, Boaz commanded his young men, saying, Let her glean even among the sheaves, and reproach her not; And let fall some of the handfuls on purpose for her, and leave them, that she may glean them, and rebuke her not.

Ruth was not out to grab all she could but to work as hard as she could. And Boaz was out to bless this damsel. She was even allowed to glean among the sheaves and not just gather what had fallen to the ground.

God has called each of his children to work in his harvest field. And he sees to it that his workers are left "handfuls on purpose" as a great encouragement along the way. I am never disappointed when I ask Jesus to leave "handfuls on purpose."

2:17 So she gleaned in the field until evening, and beat out that she had gleaned; and it was about an ephah of barley.

Imagine that she gleaned from morning to evening and then beat out what she had gleaned! That was no small task, my friend. She was accustomed to hard work and didn't back away from it although she must have been pretty "beat" herself.

An ephah equaled a bushel which was quite a large amount for a young damsel to pick in one day.

2:18-20 And she took it up, and went into the city. And her mother-in-law saw what she had gleaned; and she brought out and gave to her what she had reserved after she was satisfied. And her mother-in-law said unto her, Where hast thou gleaned today? And where wroughtest thou? Blessed be he that did take knowledge of thee. And she showed her mother-in-law with whom she had wrought, and said, The man's name whom I wrought today is Boaz. And Naomi said unto her daughter-in-law, Blessed be he of the Lord who hath not withheld his kindness to the living and to the dead. And Naomi said unto her, The man is near of kin unto us, one of our next of kinsmen.

When referring to Boaz as kin, Naomi used the personal pronouns "us" and "our" signifying that Ruth was indeed a part of her family. And she acknowledge that God was working through Boaz to bless them.

The attraction between Boaz and Ruth was not something orchestrated by Naomi. She was not working to manipulate the circumstance. Naomi wasn't the one who sent Ruth to the field of Boaz; God was! He was leading, guiding, and directing all the way without their

156

knowing. Yes, that's our God who works everything after the counsel of his own good will.

Naomi perceived it was the hand of the Lord and gave him praise for his kindness. She also acknowledged Boaz as one of their next of kin without saying he was a near-kinsman. Perhaps she was aware that there was another kinsman closer in relation than Boaz.

Ruth, not having been schooled in Mosaic Law, was unaware of the function of a kinsman redeemer. According to the law, a near-kinsman could redeem land, an individual, and/or a widow, but he was not obligated to do so. **Deuteronomy 25:5-10**

2:21 And Ruth, the Moabitess, said, He said unto me also, Thou shalt keep close by my young men, until they have ended my harvest.

Ruth excitedly told Naomi that the blessing of Boaz was to continue throughout the six weeks of harvest. Neither had any idea that this blessing would continue well beyond even that.

2:22 And Naomi said unto Ruth, her daughter-in-law, It is good, my daughter, that thou go out with his maidens, that they meet thee not in any other field.

Naomi advised Ruth to stay where she had found favor. It's good for us to seek God's favor to accomplish his purposes and to appreciate it when it is granted.

2:23 So she kept close by the maidens of Boaz to glean until the end of barley harvest and of wheat harvest, and dwelt with her mother-in-law.

Ruth had about six weeks to demonstrate who she was. How her arms, legs, and back muscles ached as she labored under the hot sun. But she continued working without complaint. She stayed with Naomi without exhibiting self-seeking interest. Her focus and concern was to work while the harvest was ripe. This, of course, should be our focus too.

John 9:4 records the words of Jesus as he taught his disciples saying, "I must work the works of him that sent me, while it is day; the night cometh, when no man can work."

Jesus spoke these words written in **John 4:35**, "Say not ye, There are yet four months, and then cometh harvest? Behold, I say unto you, Lift up your eyes, and look on the fields; for they are white already to harvest."

An evangelist was heard saying that all people, regardless of nationality or skin color, have white palms. He told of African crusades where he saw multitudes lifting up their hands in worship and said it looked like waves of wheat in a field.

Matthew 9:37-38 quotes Jesus as saying, "Then saith he unto his disciples, The harvest truly is plenteous, but the laborers are few. Pray ye, therefore, the Lord of the harvest, that he will send forth laborers into his harvest."

Working in God's harvest field can be quite a labor, but at the same time, it's quite an honor and well worth the effort.

Ruth
Chapter 3

3:1 Then Naomi, her mother-in-law, said unto her, My daughter, shall I not seek rest for thee, that it might go well with thee?

The first word is, "Then." That's important because only after the harvest had ended, then and only then, did Naomi ask Ruth about seeking "rest," meaning a husband, for her. Also, keep in mind that seeking a husband for Ruth was Naomi's idea.

3:2-3 And now is not Boaz of our kindred, with whose maidens thou wast? Behold, he winnoweth barley tonight in the threshing floor. Wash thyself, therefore, and anoint thyself, and put thy raiment upon thee, and get thee down to the floor; but make not thyself known unto the man, until he shall have done eating and drinking.

Naomi had ample opportunity to observe both Ruth and Boaz. She gave Ruth five instructions in verse 3:3 alone; all of which she obeyed.

** The following notes are from "A Study of Ruth" written by J. Vernon Magee, page 50.

"Usually a threshing floor was located on top of a hill to catch any wind that was blowing in order to blow away the chaff. The clay soil was packed to a hard smooth surface, and ordinarily it was circular with rocks placed around it. Even today this same procedure is being used.

In the late afternoon, a breeze comes up and blows until sundown and sometimes goes on until midnight. As long as the breeze is blowing the people will thresh. Sheaves of grain were spread on the floor and trampled by oxen drawing a sled. Then the people took a flail and threw the grain up into the air so that the chaff would be blown away and the good grain would be there on the threshing floor. When the wind died down, whether it be at sundown, nine o'clock, midnight, or whatever time it was, they held a great religious feast. And at this season of the year all the families came up and camped around the threshing floor, which meant there were many people present. After the feast was over, the men would sleep around the grain. Since the threshing floor was circular, they would put their heads toward the grain and their feet would stick out like spokes. They slept that way to protect the grain from thieves and animals.

It was a time of feasting and of thanking God for an abundant harvest. Imagine what a sight that was on the hilltop at night looking up into the heavens and singing and praising the same God we worship today."

Now back again to our study of Ruth:

3:4 And it shall be, when he lieth down, that thou shall mark the place where he shall lie, and thou shall go in, and uncover his feet, and lay thee down; and he will tell thee what thou shall do.

Likewise, when we come to rest at the feet of Jesus, he will tell us what to do. According to Mosaic Law, Boaz could not redeem Ruth until she sought redemption. We, too, must discern our need and seek the Redeemer who shed his precious Blood for all. Also, according to the law, the near-kinsman was not obligated to redeem.

3:5-7 And she said unto her, All that thou sayest unto me I will do. And she went down unto the floor, and did all that her mother-in-law bade her. And when Boaz had eaten and drunk, and his heart was merry, he went to lie down at the end of the heap of corn: and she came softly, and uncovered his feet, and laid down.

Let's keep in mind that Ruth followed Naomi's instruction when she uncovered his feet to make her presence known. She was not instructed to snuggle up to him and she didn't.

Wow! The harvest had ended, the feasting and worshiping had ended, and her redemption was nigh at hand! We can only imagine the overwhelming joy when God's harvest is ended and Jesus comes for his Bride!

Ruth had come to trust in the God of Israel. How her heart must have pounded as she heard and saw the grateful jubilation of his people. However, she knew that as a Moabite, she would not be welcomed in such a celebration. Not yet, that is.

Ruth "came softly" unto Boaz. My, what a manner this young damsel had. No wonder he loved her.

And, now for the crescendo of this beautiful love story.

3:8-9 And it came to pass at midnight, that the man was afraid, and turned himself; and, behold, a woman lay at his feet. And he said, Who art thou? And she answered, I am Ruth thine handmaid. Spread, therefore, thy skirt over thine handmaid; for thou art a near-kinsman.

Talk about direct and to the point! In one sentence she identified herself, acknowledged Boaz as a near-kinsman, and made her request. Her one sentence put the ball in his court so to speak. And, to be perfectly honest, that's exactly where he wanted it to be. He desired nothing more than to perform the duty of a near-kinsman to Ruth. He loved that girl. He wanted her for his own.

3:10-11 And he said, Blessed be thou of the Lord, my daughter: for thou hast shown more kindness in the latter end than at the beginning, inasmuch as thou followedst not young men, whether rich or poor. And now, my daughter, fear not; I will do to thee all that thou requirest: for all the city of my people doth know that thou art a virtuous woman.

163

Wow! This unsuspecting startled man was awakened at midnight by a foreign woman asking to be redeemed. You couldn't ask for a more dramatic scene. His response put the icing on this cake. Though Ruth did not seek the praise of Boaz, he lavished unsolicited tribute on her when he said, " ... for all the city doth know that thou art a virtuous woman." By her actions, she had earned his full approval and the approval of others.

Boaz spoke kindly and called her "my daughter" twice and admonished her to "fear not." What calm must have flooded her soul.

We are given a definition of a virtuous woman in **Proverbs 31**. Verses 10-13 echo what Boaz found in Ruth, "Who can find a virtuous woman? For her price is far above rubies. The heart of her husband doth safely trust in her, so that he shall have no need of spoil (concern). She will do him good, and not evil, all the days of her life."

This kinsman redeemer wasn't looking for a woman to display as his own personal goddess or trophy wife. He wasn't looking for a wife who would make him the envy of all the men in town. In fact, he wasn't looking for a wife at all.

3:12 And now it is true that I am thy near-kinsman; howbeit there is a kinsman nearer than I.

164

It's apparent that Boaz already knew he was a near-kinsman and that there was another near-kinsman even closer who would have the first option. This other kinsman may have been Elimelech's brother. At any rate, this other near-kinsman was a fly in the ointment so to speak.

3:13 Tarry this night, and it shall be in the morning, that if he will perform unto thee the part of a kinsman, well; let him do the kinsman's part. But if he will not do the part of a kinsman to thee, then will I do the part of a kinsman to thee, as the Lord liveth. Lie down until morning.

Well, I wrote that Ruth's request was rather direct but Boaz's response was even more direct. He gave an honest and straight forward assessment and stated his intentions. That's amazing for any man awakened at midnight by a damsel at his feet asking to be redeemed.

Though there was an obstacle, this smitten near-kinsman was ready to take immediate action, and he confirmed it with an oath. I like Boaz. He was a man of his word and wanted to do things "decently and in order" according to the law of God.

Out of concern for her safety, he implored Ruth twice to stay at his feet until morning. True enough, they both lied down until morning, but I would venture to say that neither got much sleep wondering how the matter would work out. Their thoughts must have run the entire gamut of emotions. This young foreign widow was assured she would become a bride without being assured who the groom would be. I imagine that few women have found themselves in such a perplexing situation.

Oh, and there's someone else who probably spent a sleepless night: Naomi. When Ruth didn't return from her errand, Naomi must have wondered what had transpired.

Before the foundation of the world, it was God's will to unite these two in marriage knowing their union would produce the godly seed he desired. One element that makes this story so breath-taking is that neither Boaz nor Ruth knew how God would work it out. But, work it out, he did! When it's his will, he makes the way. He is doing the same in your life today, though he may choose to not allow you to see all he is working for your good. In time you will, and you will rejoice with joy unspeakable.

By Boaz's own words, we know that he was held in suspense regarding the outcome. He was not boasting of achieving his heart's desire; a virtuous bride. He was left to wonder just as we are at times.

Proverbs 27:1 Boast not thyself of tomorrow; for thou knowest not what a day may bring forth.

Let's not pass this scene without more consideration of Ruth. Her life had not been a bed of roses. Born into paganism, marrying a foreigner, and widowed at an early age, she left her homeland to follow her mother-in-law and her mother-in-law's God who had become her God. She was a stranger in a strange land when she encountered a strange law. The kinsman-redeemer law was news to her, and the existence of another near-

166

kinsman was news to her. But the Lord had determined that all of Ruth's life would be filled with his Good News! We can truly appreciate the sincere love Ruth had for the God of Israel who works all things together for the good of those who love him.

3:14-15 And she lay at his feet until morning; and she rose up before one could know another. And he said, Let it not be known that a woman came into the floor. Also, he said, Bring the veil that thou hast upon thee, and hold it. And when she held it, he measured six measures of barley, and laid it on her; and she went into the city.

Only men were allowed on the threshing floor at night, so Boaz discreetly ushered her away but not before heaping a blessing upon her that gave evidence to Naomi of his favor.

3:16-17 And when she came to her mother-in-law, she said, How hast thou fared, my daughter? And she told her all that the man had done to her. And she said, These six measures of barley gave he me; for he said to me, Go not empty unto thy mother-in-law.

Boaz honored Naomi, too, by sending the grain gift. You may recall that Naomi had said the Lord had brought her home empty. No, Naomi, you didn't come home empty. You came home with a young pagan girl who loved you and who was right there by your side. And, Boaz, as God's instrument of blessing, would see to it that you wouldn't be empty. The great God that we love and serve did all of this through the love of the young pagan girl from Moab!

3:18 Then said she, Sit still, my daughter, until thou know how the matter will fall; for the man will not be in rest, until he have finished the thing this day.

In each and every situation, after we have done the will of God, we must wait and see how the matter will go.

Paul, while a prisoner of Nero, wrote:
Philippians 2:23 ... as soon as I see how it will go with me.

Some may feel they have to know minute by minute exactly what's going on in their own lives, but in reality we all have to wait and "see how it will go with me." (Smile)

Ruth may have taken a long nap after being awake half the night, learning Boaz wanted her for his own, and then learning of another near-kinsman. That's a good deal to process in less than twenty-four hours.

Naomi understood that Boaz would take immediate action to do all things according to the law of God. The scripture states, "until he has finished the thing." At Naomi's direction, Ruth had initiated the procedure. Boaz was willing and able. He would see to it that the matter was finished. Now that Ruth has claimed him, he is free to move and move he did!

When Jesus purchased us by his shed Blood, he said, 'It is finished." The incalculable price for the redemption of mankind had been paid in full by the Lamb of God.

168

We gladly claim him as our near-kinsman redeemer and draw night unto him just as Ruth drew nigh to Boaz.

Let's note that throughout this beautiful love story Naomi, Ruth, and Boaz did not know that the Sovereign God of all creation was working the entire matter out to his satisfaction. For them, the outcome was in doubt. As you know from experience, the Blessed Controller requires his children to walk by faith and not by sight.

Ruth
Chapter 4

4:1 Then went up Boaz to the gate, and sat him down there, and, behold, the kinsman of whom Boaz spoke came by, unto whom he said, Ho, such a one! Turn aside, sit down here. And he turned aside, and sat down.

This word "Then" struck me as interesting. Two of the four chapters in this love story begin with this word. The "Then" used as the first word in Chapter Three begins to tell us what Naomi did after Ruth had finished gleaning. She next suggested a husband might be appropriate for Ruth. The second "Then" was used to begin Chapter Four where we learn Boaz proceeded with the redemption process after Ruth made known to him her desire to be redeemed. Naomi, Ruth, and Boaz were all in the will of God without knowing God was moving providentially to accomplish his best.

And, speaking of God moving providentially, imagine the coincidence of the other kinsman approaching the gate as Boaz waited for him. This fellow thought he was only walking into town. He had no inkling that he would be called upon to make a decision that would set the course of history. A similar event may occur in your life today. Much of our personal experience can be determined by our choices. (Say "ouch" or "amen").

Boaz was not out scouting the countryside for this unnamed kinsman. When we are about our Father's business, we don't have to worry about being in the right place at the right time. Father takes care of all the details.

The "gate" was located at the entrance of the walled city. It was the place where men resorted for legal business, conversation, bargaining, and news. Boaz wasted no time in going to the spot where the redemption of Ruth could be settled - just as Jesus always journeyed toward Jerusalem to accomplish our redemption.

4:2 And he took ten men of the elders of the city, and said, Sit ye down here. And they sat down.

Boaz chose ten men to give testimony of how the matter was settled between him and the other kinsman. Some have speculated that the other kinsman was Elimelech's brother. The Bible doesn't make the relationship known; so apparently, it is not something we need to know.

4:3-4 And he said unto the kinsman, Naomi, that is come again out of the country of Moab, selleth a parcel of land, which was our brother Elimelech's; And I thought to tell thee, saying, Buy it before the inhabitants, and before the elders of my people. If thou wilt redeem it, redeem it; but if thou wilt not redeem it, then tell me, that I may know; for there is none to redeem it beside thee, and I am after thee. And he said, I will redeem it.

Boaz informed the unsuspecting kinsman that Naomi desired to sell her husband's property. This would not actually be a sale but more of a long-term lease until another year of Jubilee.

The pre-planned strategy of Boaz was to state that the property of Elimelech needed to be redeemed, saying, "**...** for there is none to redeem it before thee."

The other kinsman represented the law given by Moses which couldn't redeem lost humanity. Boaz represented our Blessed Redeemer whose Blood was shed once for all. (**Hebrews 10:10**)

According to the law, the property had to be redeemed before witnesses. Boaz held his peace as he presented the matter before the kinsman and ten witnesses. My, my how his heart must have quaked when the kinsman agreed to redeem the property. Oh, but wait, this property came with some lagniappe (an extra bonus).

Boaz did not desire the property; only the lagniappe that came with it. He may have been surprised at the other kinsman's willingness to redeem. This willingness may have been caused by him wanting to be honorable before the witnesses.

4:5 Then said Boaz, What day thou buyest the field of the hand of Naomi, thou must buy it also of Ruth, the Moabitess, the wife of the dead, to raise up the name of the dead upon his inheritance.

Boaz was quick to point out that Ruth would be an additional obligation and that she was a Moabite. He knew full well what this would mean to the other kinsman; because, according to **Deuteronomy 23:3**, a

Moabite was forbidden to enter into the congregation of the Lord. The kinsman also knew that redeeming Ruth would mean he was required to be a husband to her.

How the heart of Boaz must have raced as he thought of the young damsel he loved who had spent the night at his feet longing to become his bride.

4:6 And the kinsman said, I cannot redeem it for myself, lest I mar mine own inheritance. Redeem thou my right for thyself; for I cannot redeem it.

Well, this other fellow, though not given any advance warning, didn't need any time in making his decision. In one swift moment, he assessed the cost and determined it was too great. Just as the law could not redeem, this kinsman could not redeem.

Thank God that our near-kinsman counted the cost, left his home in glory, and became the spotless Lamb of God in order to redeem his Bride.

The inheritance reserved for the other kinsman's children would be diminished, and, because he didn't love Ruth, he wasn't willing for that to happen.

You know, love was the reason Jesus left the portals of glory to redeem his Bride. He loved her enough to suffer and die while despising the shame of the cross.

4:7-8 Now this was the manner in former times in Israel concerning redeeming and concerning changing, to confirm all things: a man took off his shoe, and gave it to his neighbor; and this was a testimony in Israel.

Therefore, the kinsman said unto Boaz, Buy it for thyself. So he drew off his shoe.

This was indeed an unusual way of signifying a refusal to redeem and of transferring ownership. Instead of "throwing in the towel," he took off his shoe and gave it to Boaz to seal the deal before ten witnesses. Receiving this man's shoe meant that Boaz was now legally married to Ruth. The unnamed man was not disgraced by his inability or unwillingness to redeem. It was a win/win.

When Jesus dismissed his Spirit on Calvary, he said, "It is finished," meaning the redemption of man had been accomplished. His shed Blood had purchased his Bride.

4:9 And Boaz said unto the elders, and unto all the people, Ye are witnesses this day, that I have bought all that was Elimelech's, and all that was Chilion's and Mahlon's of the hand of Naomi.

4:10 Moreover Ruth, the Moabitess, the wife of Mahlon, have I purchased to be my wife, to raise up the name of the dead upon his inheritance, that the name of the dead be not cut off from among his brethren, and from the gate of his place. Ye are witnesses this day.

Boaz clearly stated his intentions as he acknowledged what he had done. He was not concerned about how much it cost. He was not reluctant to marry a Moabite. He had accomplished Ruth's redemption according to the law.

4:11-12 And all the people who were in the gate, and the elders, said, We are witnesses. The Lord make the woman who is come into thine house like Rachel and like Leah, which two did build the house of Israel, and do thou worthily in Ephrathah, and be famous in Bethlehem; And let thine house be like the house of Perez, whom Tamar bore unto Judah, of the seed which the Lord shall give thee of this young woman.

Boaz and Ruth were given the blessing of the elders and the others at the gate. Truly the favor of the Lord was extended to them both. Ruth was referred to as a "young woman." We have no way of knowing her age but we do know that she became who she was by loving God and making right choices during very stressful times.

4:13 So Boaz took Ruth and she was his wife; and when he went in unto her, the Lord gave her conception, and she bare a son.

So here we have a man fulfilling the duty of a kinsman, becoming a husband, and producing the godly seed the Lord desired. It's interesting that Ruth had no children in nearly ten years of marriage to Mahlon. Now, with the blessing of God, she had a son who will be as Naomi's grandson. She didn't envision any of this as she made her heartfelt decision to cling unto Naomi and to her God. Neither can you envision the plans God has for you.

Consider the words written for us in:

Jeremiah 29:11 For I know the thoughts that I think toward you, saith the Lord, thoughts of peace, and not of evil, to give you an expected end.

Ruth 4:14-15 And the women said unto Naomi, Blessed be the Lord, which hath not left thee this day without a kinsman, that his name may be famous in Israel. And he shall be unto thee a restorer of thy life, and a nourisher in thine old age; for thy daughter-in-law, who loveth thee, who is better to thee than seven sons, hath born him.

The women of Bethlehem-Judah were quick to praise God for blessing Naomi with a kinsman, with Ruth, and their son. The disturbing lack of gratitude by Naomi is alarming. The other women acknowledged that Ruth was better to her than seven sons. No words of gratefulness are ever ascribed to Naomi.

No one could have imagined the great and awesome things that God was doing. They could not have known that this heathen girl from God's "washpot" had carried the future of Israel in her womb. Talk about going from rags to riches! This young Moabite girl did just that. And that's exactly what happens to anyone who leaves the world behind and follows Christ to become a part of his redeemed Bride.

4:16-17 And Naomi took the child, and laid it in her bosom, and became nurse to it. And the women, her neighbors, gave him a name, saying, There is a son born to Naomi; and they called his name Obed: he is the father of Jesse, the father of David.

176

The rejoicing townswomen named the baby Obed, which means "servant or worshiper." He was to become the grandfather of King David.

As already noted, Naomi displayed a shocking lack of gratitude. God had decreed the near-kinsman law as a way of protecting widows and of keeping land within the family. Had Naomi been widowed and childless in any other country or people group, she would not have had the benefit of the kinsman law. I wonder if that thought ever occurred to her.

Life's adversities can cause someone to become bitter or better. Hearts can differ. It's been said that the heat that melts wax will harden steel. Likewise, some hearts remain tender and sensitive, whereas some become calloused and hard.

4:18-22 Now these are the generations of Perez: Perez begot Hezron, and Hezron begot Ram, and Ram begot Amminadab, and Amminadab begot Salmon, and Salmon begot Boaz, and Boaz, begot Obed, and Obed begot Jesse, and Jesse begot David.

This genealogy listing is very important and provides a clear link to the family of King David to the tribe of Judah from which our Lord descended. As noted earlier, God further honored Ruth by listing her as one of the four women named in the Lord's genealogy found in **Matthew 1:3-16**. What an honor!

I recently heard a radio ad for a new translation Bible that had been modernized to omit all unnecessary words. It boasted that among the omitted verses were the begets. My heart sank as I thought of the names listed in **Matthew 1:3-16** and **Luke 3:23-38**. Even an overview of their lives provide a wealth of insightful revelation. The Bible wouldn't be complete without the begets. And remember the instruction given in:

Revelation 22:19 And if any man shall take away from the words of the book of this prophecy, God shall take away his part out of the book of life, and out of the holy city, and from the things which are written in this book.

Included in the words spoken by Hannah and recorded in **1st Samuel 2:3** are these, " ... for the Lord is a God of knowledge, and by him are actions are weighed."

It has been said that actions speak louder than words. The four chapters in the story of Ruth show the actions of every person involved. We were told at the beginning that Ruth loved her mother-in-law, and she showed it by her actions - that she chose Naomi's God to be her God and showed it by her actions, she chose to work hard without complaining, and she was obedient to her mother-in-law and showed it all by her actions.

We were told early on that Boaz was a wealthy man. By his actions, we learned that he was a man of integrity who upheld the law. He freely divested himself of his personal wealth to redeem his bride.

We can understand why Boaz redeemed this virtuous young damsel to be his bride. But a baffling question for Christians is: Why God would send his only Son to suffer and die on the cross for our sins when there is none worthy among men? The answer is love.

John 3:16 For God so loved the world, that he gave his only begotten Son, that whosoever believeth in him should not perish but have everlasting life.

1st John 4:9-10 In this was manifested the love of God toward us, that God sent his only begotten Son into the world, that we might live through him. Herein is love, not that we loved God, but that he loved us, and sent his Son to be the propitiation (substitute) for our sins.

Galatians 3:13 Christ hath redeemed us from the curse of the law, being made a curse for us; for it is written, Cursed is everyone that hangeth on a tree ...

Titus 2:14 (Jesus) who gave himself for us that he might redeem us from all iniquity, and purify unto himself a people of his own, zealous of good works.

And here's a favorite verse:
1st Peter 1:21 Who by him do believe in God, who raised him up from the dead and gave him glory that your faith and hope might be in God.

BOOK OF JONAH
A Misunderstood Man

There may not be a more maligned Bible prophet than Jonah and that is a large part of the reason this study was researched, written, and published. And the Book of Jonah may be the one Bible book that only mentions one person's name in addition to God. It's a revelation of our merciful God working to draw unworthy people unto himself. He is still doing that today.

My heart reacts strongly when someone "rags out" on a Bible individual who lived in a time of great adversity and who was called by God to do seemingly impossible things; so it was with Jonah. He was not a cartoon caricature, though some have depicted him as such. The events in his life covered in these four chapters were not intended to be viewed as a sitcom script. His name means "dove." The dove has been a symbol of peace and purify since the days of Noah.

Jonah was a prophet of Israel who lived 800 years B.C. He was the first prophet sent out from Israel, and the first sent to Gentiles. Israel was the world's trade center and all roads of commerce went through there. Prophets sent messages out from Israel to other nations. Jonah was called upon by God to break that tradition.

The site thought to be Jonah's burial place was destroyed by ISIS Muslim militants in Mosul, Iraq Thursday, July 25, 2014. Knowing this site to be revered by both Jews and Christians made it an irresistible target for the terrorists.

Nineveh was the capital city of the nation of Assyria and was twenty-seven miles around. The Assyrians were very brutal and showed no mercy to those they conquered. Their soldiers would move as a slow mincing army devouring everything in its path. History records that whole villages would commit suicide rather than be conquered. Assyrians would rape and torture the women before killing them with their children. Men would be buried in the sand with only their necks extended. Their tongues would then be stretched and impaled with arrows driven into the sand. They were left to become the prey of wild animals. It is recorded that some would become insane and howl during the night until their life was gone.

Is it any wonder that Jonah resisted God's order for him to go to Nineveh, capital of Assyria? There is a real possibility that Jonah had vivid memories of his own grandmothers, mother, and sisters being raped and tortured by the Assyrians. Perhaps his own father and other men known to him had met terrible deaths at the hands of the merciless Assyrians.

How would Jonah be received by his own countryman after returning from his mission? How could he face his own people who had been forced to pay tribute to the Assyrians for four generations? God had purposed Jonah's mission to have a reforming effect upon the Israelites after his return.

Founded by Noah's grandson, Nimrod, the city of Nineveh was located on the Tigris River. Dating the time of Nineveh's destruction is difficult since the Assyrians did not date years with numbers but, instead, named the years for their rulers. When the city was excavated between 1843-45, it was learned that the surrounding walls were 100' high and 40' thick making it a virtual fortress. Two chariots could travel side by side on top of the wall offering further protection. No army was known to have penetrated this great city, but Jonah did by only speaking the eight words given to him by God!

Like most Old Testament books, it was written in the third person. Many believe it was written by Jonah himself.

One commentator stated the following assessment of Jonah: "He was a proud, self-centered egotist, willful, pouting, jealous, blood-thirsty, a good patriot, and a lover of Israel without proper respect for God or love for his enemies."

If these are your thoughts too, it is hoped that this study will persuade you to reconsider. (smile)

The Bible gives the unvarnished version of actual people and events that can be historically proven for those unbelieving or skeptical. Our Jonah was not the prima donna of prophets, but, just as Jesus validated his ministry, so will this lesson.

Matthew 12:39-41 But he answered and said unto them, An evil and adulterous generation seeketh after a sign, and there shall no sign be given to it, but the sign of the prophet Jonah; For as Jonah was three days and three nights in the belly of the great fish, so shall the Son of man be three days and three nights in the heart of the earth. The men of Nineveh shall rise in judgment with this generation, and shall condemn it; because they repented at the preaching of Jonah; and, behold, a greater than Jonah is here.

182

Jonah
Chapter One

1:1-2 Now the word of the Lord came upon Jonah, the son of Amittai, saying, Arise, go to Nineveh, that great city, and cry against it; for their wickedness is come up before me.

In this beginning statement, we are told that the Lord "came to Jonah." It does not say that Jonah was seeking guidance and direction from the Lord. God spoke specific direction to his servant without telling him what his mission would be or what the results would be. He is still doing that today.

1:3 But Jonah rose up to flee unto Tarshish from the presence of the Lord, and went down to Joppa, and he found a ship going to Tarshish; so he paid the fare, and went down into it, to go with them unto Tarshish from the presence of the Lord.

Verse three begins with, "But Jonah," verse four begins with, "But the Lord," as does verse five. Jonah was to learn that when God speaks there are "no ifs, ands, or buts about it." Jonah fled from only a partial revelation of God's will and went in the opposite direction toward Tarshish in the south part of Spain some 2,500 miles from Nineveh.

He had not expected to hear such instruction from the Lord, and it was not something he was glad to hear. Has something similar happened to you as you endeavor to do his will? I dare say that, if it hasn't, it will. We learn over and over that God's ways are not our ways.

"From the presence of the Lord" is stated twice in this one verse. As a prophet of God, he must have known that he could not flee from God's presence. His fleeing may indicate total shock at what he knew God had said.

We cannot be led by which doors open as though everything is "falling into place." Circumstances may be "falling into place" in order for us to be corrected by God.

Everything went Jonah's way as he fled from the presence of the Lord. He may have felt that his decision to flee was somehow being blessed. He went to Joppa, found a ship going to the furthermost from Nineveh, bought a ticket, and got on board expecting to be taken far away.

Proverbs 19:21 There are many devices in a man's heart; nevertheless, the counsel of the Lord, that shall stand.

God understood the heart and thoughts of Jonah. He understands ours, too. God knew that after a frightening attention-getting detour, Jonah would be persuaded to go to Nineveh.

1:4 But the Lord sent out a great wind into the sea, and there was a mighty tempest in the sea, so that the ship was in danger of being broken.

Many of the forty-eight scriptures stating, "But the Lord" provide intriguing insight into the interventions of God. After all, he has always been God, and he will always be God. He is God alone, and he is God enough.

"But the Lord," tells us that God disrupted Jonah's plans in order to accomplish his own. (Hint: He will do that in your life's journey, too.) It was God who sent a "great wind." This is the first of eight times that something "great" is mentioned in the four chapters of Jonah. You will enjoy finding the others as we continue.

Jonah's storm was a very great and terrifying storm. It was not an ordinary storm. If you find yourself in the midst of a tempest with storms raging all around, or if you feel you are being tossed to and fro, consider the possibility that the Lord is using the turbulence to get you back on course with his desire and purpose. The Lord had sent this terrible storm to get Jonah back on track, and it did just that!

Philippians 2:13 ... for it is God who worketh in you both to will and to do of his good pleasure.

Here's some seasoned advice: Do not rush to relieve the storm situations in someone's life without seeking the Lord first. By rescuing the perishing (also known as the Jesus Complex,) you could be frustrating the purposes of God and delaying his plan for their life.

1:5 The mariners were afraid, and cried every man unto his god, and cast forth the wares that were in the ship into the sea, to lighten them of it. But Jonah was gone down into the sides of the ship; and he lay, and was fast asleep.

These men were veteran mariners who knew their lives were in jeopardy. They cried unto their "little g gods." But Jonah was "fast asleep" feeling fully justified or "just-as I'd" done nothing wrong."

1:6 So the shipmaster came to him, and said unto him, What meanest thou, O sleeper? Arise, call upon thy God, if so be that God will think upon us, that we perish not.

Even the ship's captain implored Jonah to pray. Like anyone fleeing from the presence of God, Jonah didn't feel much like praying. He didn't pray until he found himself in the belly of the great fish.

1:7 And they said everyone to his fellow, Come, and let us cast lots that we may know for whose cause this evil is upon us. So they cast lots, and the lot fell upon Jonah.

Well, Jonah, you can run but you can't hide. I wonder what he thought as the lots were cast, and I wonder what he would have done had the lot fallen on another man.

Proverbs 16:33 The lot is cast into the lap, but the whole disposing thereof is of the Lord.

Numbers 32:23 ... and be sure your sins will find you out.

The Blessed Controller has a way of bringing out what he wants to be brought out, my friend.

1:8 Then they said unto him, Tell us, we pray thee, for whose cause this evil is upon us. What is thine occupation? And from where comest thou? What is thy country? And of what people art thou?

The frightened mariners began their interrogation and asked five questions before Jonah could even answer one. His answers only intensified their fears.

1:9-10 And he said unto them, I am a Hebrew; and I fear the Lord, the God of heaven, who hath made the sea, and the dry land. Then were the men exceedingly afraid, and said unto him, Why hast thou done this? For the men knew that he fled from the presence of the Lord, because he had told them.

The wayward prophet acknowledged that he was a Hebrew and added that he feared the Lord of heaven. Okay, Jonah, let's be perfectly honest. If you truly feared the God of the Hebrews who made the heaven, the sea, and the dry land, why did you flee from him? Your actions have spoken louder than your words. Jonah had told the mariners that he had "fled from the presence of the Lord." The word "fled" (Hebrew #1272) means to bolt suddenly. It's never good to bolt suddenly from the presence of the Lord.

187

The men, who were frightened by the storm, were now exceedingly afraid and asked question number six: Why hast thou done this? We are not told if Jonah answered the "Why" question. He may have been wondering why himself. At any rate, this colossal storm put a damper on his escape plan.

1:11-12 Then said they unto him, what shall we do for thee, that the sea may be calm for us? For the sea raged, and was tempestuous. And he said unto them, Take me up, and cast me forth into the sea; so shall the sea be calm for you; for I know that for my sake this great tempest is upon you.

With the seventh and final question, the decision of what to do was left to Jonah. Jonah felt his death would appease God. He didn't realize that his death would accomplish nothing; only his obedience would. It appears that Jonah would rather die than repent, pray, or seek the Lord. His steadfast refusal ensured greater adversity ahead for the wayward prophet.

1:13 Nevertheless, the men rowed hard to bring her to the land, but they could not; for the sea raged, and was tempestuous against them.

Amazingly, the mariners showed mercy to Jonah even though their lives were imperiled because of him. They did their best but couldn't out-row the storm. Neither can we row the boat out of harm's way for someone in rebellion against God.

1:14 Wherefore, they cried unto the Lord, and said, We beseech thee, O Lord, we beseech thee, let us not perish for this man's life, and lay not upon us innocent blood; for thou, O Lord, hast done as it pleased thee.

The men who had each called upon his own "little g god," were now calling on the God of Jonah; still we aren't told that Jonah prayed. The distressed mariners acknowledged the sovereignty of the God we know who is God alone.

It's a fact that others often suffer when someone rebels against God.

1:15 So they took up Jonah, and cast him forth into the sea; and the sea ceased from its raging.

Jonah had stated (verse 1:9) that his God created the sea. And, now, after having been cast into it and the storm ceasing, Jonah had no doubt that God was in control.

1:16 Then the men feared the Lord exceedingly, and offered a sacrifice unto the Lord and made vows.

This was the last mention of the ship and its crew. They may have surmised that Jonah had met his death at the hands of an angry God. They could not have guessed what God had assigned to Jonah. And we can only wonder if their coming to fear the God of Jonah had a lasting effect on their lives. The wayward prophet would soon learn that he could neither out-run nor out-swim God.

1:17 Now the Lord had prepared a great fish to swallow up Jonah. And Jonah was in the belly of the fish three days and three nights.

Everything was made ready for Jonah in advance. The great fish (not whale) was in the exact spot it needed to be to swallow the cast-over Jonah. We aren't told if the mariners witnessed the event.

After being in the belly of the great fish three days and three nights, something wonderful happened.

First, let's consider this:

Before beginning chapter two, if the account of Jonah and the great fish seems a bit too fishy, let's review a few documented accounts of others who have shared Jonah's bizarre experience and who lived to tell about it.

The following reports are gleaned from writings of Dr. J. Vernon McGee.

"One such survivor couldn't share his experience though: a dog, who according to Dr. Ransome Harvey was lost overboard from a ship. He was found in the head of a whale six days later, alive and barking.

The famous French scientist, M. de Parville wrote of James Bartley, who in the region of the Falkland Islands near South America, was supposed to have drowned at sea. Two days after his disappearance, the sailors

190

caught a whale. When it was cut up, much to their surprise they found their missing friend alive but unconscious inside the whale. He revived and enjoyed good health following his misadventure.

Dr. Harry Rimmer, then President of the Research Bureau of Los Angeles, wrote of another case reported in the Literary Digest of an account of an English sailor who was swallowed by a gigantic Rhinodon in the English Channel. Trying to harpoon the monstrous shark, the sailor fell overboard, and before he could be rescued, the shark turned and engulfed him.

Forty-eight hours after the accident, the fish was sighted and slain. When the sailors opened the shark, they were amazed to find the man unconscious but alive! He was rushed to a hospital where he was found to be suffering from shock alone and was released a few hours later.

The article concluded by saying the man was on exhibit in a London Museum at a shilling admittance fee; being advertised as "The Jonah of the Twentieth Century."

In 1926 Dr. Rimmer met this man and wrote that his physical appearance was odd; his body was devoid of hair and patches of yellowish-brown color covered his entire skin.

There are at least two known monsters of the deep who could have easily swallowed Jonah and neither have any teeth. They are the Balaenoptera Musculus or sulphur bottom whale, and the Rhinodon Typicus or whale shark. They feed in an interesting way by opening their enormous mouths, submerging their lower jaw, and rushing through the water at terrific speed. After

191

straining out the water, they swallow whatever is left. A sulphur bottom whale, one hundred feet long, was captured off Cape Cod in 1933. His mouth was ten to twelve feet wide – so big he could have easily swallowed a horse. These whales have four to six compartments in their stomachs, in any one of which a colony of men could find free lodging. They might even have a choice of rooms, for in the head of this whale is an air storage chamber, an enlargement of the nasal sinus, often measuring seven feet high, seven feet wide, and fourteen feet long. If he had an unwelcome guest on board who gives him a headache, the whale swims to the nearest land and gets rid of the offender as Jonah's great fish did!"

Jonah
Chapter Two

2:1 Then Jonah prayed unto the Lord, his God, out of the fish's belly.

Let's pause for a moment and relish that statement: Jonah prayed. Well, it was about time he prayed!

At the end of this chapter, it becomes clear that Jonah had been in the belly of this fish for three days and nights before praying. He may have been in a shock or even unconscious as has been reported of others with similar experiences.

2:2-3 And, said, I cried by reason of my affliction unto the Lord, and he heard me; out of the belly of hell cried I, and thou heardest my voice. For thou hast cast me into the deep, in the midst of the seas, and the floods compassed me about; all thy billows and thy waves passed over me.

Our Jonah, encased in the fish's belly prayed as many others who cried to God at the point of their greatest need. Others, like King David, who wrote:

> **Psalm 9:12** ... he forgetteth not the cry of the humble.

> **Psalm 3:4** I cried unto the Lord with my voice, and he heard me out of his holy hill.

Psalm 34:4 I sought the Lord, and he heard me, and delivered me from all my fears.

Knowing where he was and with no hope of escape, he called it "the belly of hell," a phase not used elsewhere in the Bible.

2:4-5 Then I said, I am cast out of thy sight; yet I will look again toward thine holy temple. The waters compassed me about, even to the soul; the depth closed me round about, the weeds were wrapped about my head.

In his miserable hopeless predicament, Jonah thought he would die but he still hoped to see God. He described a not-so-lovely environment.

2:6-7 I went down to the bottoms of the mountains; the earth, with its bars, was about me forever; yet hast thou brought up my life from corruption, O Lord, my God. When my soul fainted with me, I remembered the Lord; and my prayer came unto thee, into thy holy temple.

This prayer-like conversation with God is remarkable. He knows now that he cannot flee from his presence.

2:8 They that observe lying vanities forsake their own mercy.

This statement holds an interesting truth. What Jonah needed from God is what we need: mercy or unmerited

194

favor. When focused on ourselves, we are deceived by thoughts and pursuits which produce vanity and that keep us from his mercy.

2:9 But I will sacrifice unto thee with the voice of thanksgiving; I will pay that which I have vowed. Salvation is of the Lord.

Looking beyond his present circumstance, Jonah made a solemn pledge to fulfill a vow which he had made presumably while in the fish's belly. It's thought that his vow was to obey God in going to Nineveh.

All believers must obey God without knowing the specific steps he has ordered regardless of the difficulty involved. Only by going on in the path he has chosen can we see all the puzzle pieces come together.

Perhaps the most profound words in these four chapters are "Salvation is of the Lord." This is the truth that Jonah held onto and didn't "belly-ache" in the belly of the great fish.

2:10 And the Lord spoke unto the fish, and it vomited out Jonah upon dry land.

God heard Jonah's plea and spoke to the great fish without speaking to Jonah. It seems they were not yet back on speaking terms.

We know from our own experience that when God floods our soul with peace, he has heard our prayer and has moved on our behalf. Perhaps this was so with Jonah.

195

It's thought that the dry land Jonah was deposited on was Joppa, the place he trekked to while fleeing from God. Joppa, located some thirty miles northwest of Jerusalem, is mentioned ten times in the Book of Acts. Monuments erected as early as 1600 B.C. testify of its existence even then.

Jonah
Chapter Three

3:1-2 And the word of the Lord came unto Jonah the second time, saying, Arise, go unto Nineveh, that great city, and preach unto it the preaching that I bid thee.

So here the God of the second chance instructed his reluctant servant. God still didn't give him full understanding of what his assignment would be just as Paul was only given step-by-step direction after his Damascus Road encounter. You would think that a prophet would have little doubt concerning the subject matter of his message. But God says, "You go, I will show."

3:3 So Jonah arose, and went unto Nineveh, according to the word of the Lord. Now Nineveh was an exceedingly great city of three days' journey.

If Joppa was his starting point, Jonah had journeyed some 800 miles to reach Nineveh. Upon reaching Nineveh, he was met with the daunting task of preaching to an estimated 120,000 people in a city twenty-seven miles around.

3:4 And Jonah began to enter into the city a day's journey, and he cried, and said, "Yet forty days, and Nineveh shall be overthrown."

Jonah, now the first foreign missionary, spoke only the eight words given to him by God. God was responsible for the results, and he made sure these words didn't fall on deaf ears.

3:5-6 So the people of Nineveh believed God, and proclaimed a fast, and put on sackcloth, from the greatest of them even to the least of them. For the word came unto the king of Nineveh, and he arose from his throne, and he laid his robe from him, and covered himself with sackcloth, and sat in ashes.

God had gone before and prepared the hearts of these people. Trusting that their city was an impenetrable fortress, they didn't fear an enemy invasion. Jonah's eight words caused them to fear God's judgment. Their actions of fasting and wearing of sackcloth were evidence of their belief and heartfelt repentance.

NOTE: Sackcloth was a coarse material made from goat hair.

The unnamed king of this vast heathen city took off his royal apparel that had identified him as a powerful individual and put on sackcloth just as the lowest of the lowest person had. Jonah didn't seek a private audience with the king and yet his eight-word message reached the king's ears and heart. Yes, indeed, God was directing the results of Jonah's mission!

These heathen people received this foreigner's eight-word message, whereas Jesus went unto his own and his own received him not **(John 1:1)**, even after they were presented with overwhelming scriptural evidence.

When someone truly sees himself as he actually is and repents, he will begin to put off all false appearances of position, worth, and self-importance. As God graciously makes us aware of our sin and need for forgiveness and cleansing, we also become aware that he doesn't distinguish people by their earthly stature, rank, or status; only by their love for him.

1st Corinthians 8:3 But if any man love God, the same is known of him.

Jonah 3:7-8 And he (the king) caused it to be proclaimed and published through Nineveh by the decree of the king and his nobles, saying, let neither man nor beast, herd or flock, taste anything; let them not feed, nor drink water, but let man and beast be covered with sackcloth, and cry mightily unto God; yea, let them turn everyone from his evil way, and from the violence that is in their hands.

So the unnamed king, whom Jonah did not seek out, caused his words to be published throughout Nineveh. Jonah did all that he could do; God did the rest. Jonah had felt God's assignment was too much and that it was an impossible mission. Have you ever felt that way, my friend? Endeavor to obey God and to make your ways pleasing unto him; he will work everything out to his satisfaction. It's not our ability, but our availability that matters.

199

The unnamed king continued:

3:9 Who can tell if God will turn and repent, and turn away from his fierce anger, that we perish not?

These wicked people knew they weren't worthy of God's mercy and yet they sought it knowing the God of the Hebrews was the Almighty God and greatly to be feared.

3:10 And God saw their works, that they turned from their evil way; and God repented of the evil that he had said that he would do unto them, and he did it not.

God's receiving of the people's repentance resulted in the greatest move of God recorded in scripture. However, the Book of Nahum tells of God's judgment against Nineveh some hundred years later after it forsook God.

There are at least two other scriptures stating that God repented: **Genesis 6:6** and **Exodus 32:14**.

To authenticate a prophet's pronouncement, the words he speaks must be performed. Though Jonah's actual words were not performed, he was a true prophet whose words brought the results God had intended.

Jonah
Chapter Four

4:1-2 But it displeased Jonah exceedingly, and he was very angry. And he prayed unto the Lord, and said, I pray thee, O Lord, was not this my saying when I was yet in my own country. Therefore, I fled before unto Tarshish; for I knew that thou art a gracious God, and merciful, slow to anger, and of great kindness, and repentest thee of the evil.

Our reluctant prophet-missionary is more than a little displeased; more than a little angry. This is his first recorded prayer since the great fish episode. He pleaded with God to remember that even when he was in his own country, he had an understanding of God.

4:3 Therefore, now, O Lord, take, I beseech thee, my life from me; for it is better for me to die than to live.

Jonah had completed his assignment and was free to return home; but, how could he since he feared his countryman would stone him for treason?
He now knew that God would not allow him to kill himself as he thought when he volunteered to be thrown overboard, so he asked God to allow him to die. There doesn't seem to be a desire in Jonah to reach the land of eternal bliss; only a desire to end his present dilemma. Like us, Jonah was thoroughly human. (smile)

4:4 Then said the Lord, Doest thou well to be angry?

God asked Jonah to consider his own heart. By the way, when we stand before him in the judgment, the only thing that will matter is what is in our own hearts.

Throughout Jonah's ordeal, God had only spoken a few words to him. The same may happen to you. It's been said that a teacher remains silent during a test. God is a masterful teacher, fellow pilgrim.

4:5 So Jonah went out of the city, and sat on the east side of the city, and there made a booth for himself, and sat under it in the shadow, til he might see what would become of the city.

Hapless Jonah still hoped God would somehow repent of the gracious undeserved mercy he had bestowed upon Nineveh. He sat down to wait the remainder of the forty days.

4:6-7 And the Lord prepared a gourd, and made it come up over Jonah, that it might be a shadow over his head, to deliver him from his grief. So Jonah was exceedingly glad for the gourd. But God prepared a worm when the morning rose the next day, and it smote the gourd, that it withered.

By growing a gourd over Jonah, the Lord provided relief from the arid heat and demonstrated his omnipotent care. A gourd is a rather worthless plant that is kin to the squash, but it was of great value to Jonah. God demonstrated by the demise of the gourd, which was important to Jonah, that the worthless people of Nineveh were of great value to God. The worm represented Jonah who would rather smite the Assyrians than to have them turn to God and receive forgiveness.

The word "exceedingly" is a strong word used five times in the four chapters: the mariners were exceedingly afraid twice, Nineveh was an exceedingly great city, Jonah was exceedingly displeased, and Jonah was exceedingly glad for the gourd. Everyone involved had exceedingly strong emotions, but none surpassed the exceedingly great mercy of God.

4:8 And it came to pass, when the sun did rise, that God prepared a vehement east wind; and the sun beat upon the head of Jonah, that he fainted, and wished in himself to die, and said, It is better for me to die than to live.

After fainting and then reviving, the weary Jonah felt death would be a welcome remedy. Jonah's self-made shelter was no match for the God-sent storm. By the way, neither can we weather life's storms with self-made shelters. Reliance on God alone is our only shelter and is the only shelter we need.

Psalm 46:1 God is our refuge and strength, a very present help in trouble.

Throughout this saga, God was busy preparing. He prepared a great fish, a gourd, a worm, and now a vehement (hot and angry) east wind.

It is hoped that the following information concerning the east wind will interest you as it has me.

East Wind

Scripture records God sending the east wind as an instrument of judgment. We know from the following ten scriptures that the east wind brought the plague of locusts, dried the Red Sea, caused the corn to be thin and blasted (blighted), broke ships apart, withered plants, dried fountains, and was used to smite Jonah.

Genesis 41:6 And, behold, seven thin ears and blighted with the east wind sprung up after them.

Exodus 10:13 And Moses stretched forth his rod over the land of Egypt, and the Lord brought an east wind upon the land all and all that night ...

Exodus 14:21 And Moses stretched forth his hand over the sea; and the Lord caused the sea to go back by a strong east wind all that night, and made the sea dry land, and the waters were divided.

Psalm 48:7 Thou breakest the ships of Tarshish with an east wind.

Isaiah 27:8 ... he stayeth his rough wind in the day of the east wind. (God chose to temper his judgment.)

Jeremiah 18:17 I will scatter them with an east wind before the enemy; I will show them the back, and not the face, in the day of their calamity.

Ezekiel 17:10 Yes, behold, being planted, shall it prosper? Shall it not utterly wither, when the east wind toucheth it?

Ezekiel 27:26 Thy rowers have brought thee into great waters; the east wind hath broken thee in the midst of the seas.

Hosea 13:15 Though he be fruitful among his brethren, an east wind shall come, the wind of the Lord shall come up from the wilderness, and his spring shall become dry and his fountain shall be dried up ...

Okay, now we'll rejoin Jonah and the conclusion of his "learning experience."

Jonah 4:8 And it came to pass, when the sun did rise, that God prepared a vehement east wind; and the sun did beat upon the head of Jonah ...

The following verses record a curious conversation initiated by God.

4:9 And God said to Jonah, Doest thou well to be angry for the gourd? And he said, I do well to be angry, even unto death.

205

God knew Jonah's emotion without asking. Jonah felt entirely justified; something he needed to provide his only comfort had been taken by God after he had obeyed and delivered his message to Nineveh.

4:10-11 Then said the Lord, Thou hast had pity on the gourd, for which thou hast not labored, neither madest it grow; which came up in a night, and perished in a night. And should not I spare Nineveh, that great city, in which are more than six-score thousand persons that cannot discern between their right hand and their left hand; and also much cattle?

Jonah's earlier response showed the depth of his anger over losing his shade but didn't address his anger over Nineveh's repentance and acceptance by God. He would rather have died than live knowing the forgiveness of Jehovah-God had been granted to the Assyrians. Emotionally distraught and deeply wounded, Jonah had taken God's mercy as a personal insult.

The God who spared Sodom for ten righteous souls had now spared the city of Nineveh containing approximately 120,000 adults, plus children. This same God was now focused on one soul: **J o n a h**.

You may be thinking, "Ahem, the people repented, God repented, **but** the disgruntled Jonah did not repent even after private counseling by God."

Like us, neither the people of Nineveh nor Jonah were worthy of God's mercy. His mercy is always undeserved; that is what makes it mercy.

IF I WERE HUNGRY

Our Father's word is often quoted. Sadly though, it can be misquoted and misunderstood, too.

A prime example is found in Psalm 50. You may have heard someone quote only, "God owns the cattle on a thousand hill" in boasting that he will easily meet any and every need they have. That sentiment was not what the Lord had in mind when he instructed Asaph to write the following:

Psalm 50:7-11 Hear, O my people, and I will testify against thee: I am God, even thy God. I will not reprove thee for thy sacrifices or thy burnt offerings, to have been continually before me. I will take no bullock out of thy house, nor he-goats out of thy folds. For every beast of the field is mine, and <u>the cattle upon a thousand hill are mine</u>. I know all the fowls of the mountains; and the wild beasts of the field are mine.

This is written to encourage you to study surrounding scriptures and circumstances before quoting partial or isolated segments of the holy word of God.

In the above verses, God is merely saying he doesn't need anything from us since all things seen and unseen were created by him.

The psalm continues with words from his aching heart.

Psalm 50:12 If I were hungry, I would not tell thee; for the world is mine. And all the fullness thereof.

207

Those are straight-forward words from God's throbbing heart. To put it even more simply, he is saying that he knows their hearts are not with him; therefore, if he needed food or anything else, he would not tell them. What a sad commentary!

I have caused my gracious God to be sad, and the memory of it makes me hang my head in shame. When I complained that I had come a hard way in my walk. His rapid reply had a dejected sound, "I would have taught you all you needed to know but you ..." He left it to me to fill in the blank with perhaps "wouldn't or didn't." I was crushed but corrected.

In a church wedding ceremony, I sensed that something was horribly wrong. I asked the Lord what it was. There are no words to convey the sorrow in his voice when he cried, "They won't let me in."

While on the phone praying with a woman for her dying backslidden sister-in-law, the Lord disrupted my prayer by interjecting, "They call upon me in death but won't call upon me in life." The heart-wrenching sadness conveyed was too much for me to bear.

While enjoying an invigorating church worship service, I was stunned to hear the Lord lament, "People don't love me like they should." Once again, my heart quaked.

And, in yet another church during the worship service, I saw the lead guitar player's face literally drop as his shoulders drooped. He later told me that the Lord had said, "They are trying to reach me without entering in."

Yes, he is the Creator of all things and, from that perspective, you might think he doesn't need anything from his creation. But he does! Old Testament scriptures are replete with the yearnings from God's heart to be loved, understood, and sought after.

Jeremiah 9:23-24 Thus saith the LORD, let not the wise man glory in his wisdom, neither let the mighty man glory in his might, let not the rich man glory in his riches, but let him that glorieth glory in this, that he understandeth and knoweth me, that I am the LORD who exerciseth loving-kindness, judgment, and righteousness in the earth; for in such things I delight, saith the LORD.

The Lord invites his people to glory in (to boast in) the fact that they know and understand him. Marvelous. Yet, we will not know or understand him without diligently seeking.

This is written to encourage you to make knowing, loving, and understanding God your lifelong pursuit. This is accomplished through prayer, fasting, and Bible study. You have to begin sometime. Why not today?

I recall the time I walked to a neighbor's house and meekly asked, "The Old Testament was before Jesus and the New Testament was after, right?" Well, my friend that was the smallest of small steps, but at least it was a step.

God had put a hunger in my heart to know him. I have sought him since that day and have enjoyed a rewarding journey.

OUR LIMITED LIMITLESS GOD

It has been said that the Bible is God's gracious self-disclosure. And where would feeble-fallen-finite man be without his gracious self-disclosure? We acknowledge humbly that even though we have his word and his spirit resides within us, we still only grasp a thimbleful of the knowledge of God.

1st John 3:2 Beloved, now are we the sons of God, and it doth not yet appear what we shall be, but we know that, when he shall appear, we shall be like him; for we shall see him as he is.

1st Corinthians 13:12 For now we see through a glass, darkly; but then face to face: now I know in part; but then shall I know even as also I am known.

We can only enjoy imagining what it will be like to see God and to know him as he truly is. Oh, what a day that will be! Anticipating entrance into his kingdom is joy unspeakable.

In the meantime, our Creator-God is only restricted by the limits he imposes on himself and by those he chooses to allow man to place.

Here are some scripture examples:

Genesis 6:-6-7 (When he saw the wickedness of man) And it repented God that he made man on the earth, and it grieved him at his heart. And the Lord said, I will destroy man whom I have created from the face of the earth both man, and beast, and the creeping thing ...

Deuteronomy 5:29 O that there was such a heart in them, that they would fear me, and keep my commandments, that it might be well with them, and with their children forever!

Numbers 14:11 And the Lord said unto Moses, How long will this people provoke me? And how long will it be before they believe me, for all the signs which I have shown among them?

Of course, the Creator is not limited by what his creation does or doesn't do. He is never out of options.

Isaiah 42:14 I have for a long time held my peace; I have been still, and restrained myself.

Isaiah 48:18 Oh, that thou hadst harkened unto my commandments! Then thy peace had been like a river, and thy righteousness like the waves of the sea ...

As Creator, he could have chosen an infinite number of ways to cause people to harken to his commandments. He chose, instead, to withhold what would have been theirs had they done so: peace and righteousness.

Psalm 81:13 O, that my people had harkened unto me, and Israel had walked in my ways! I should soon have subdued their enemies, and turned my hand against their adversaries.

Their enemies were all who opposed the one true God. How God wanted a people of his own; his ecclesia! When his people refused to walk in his ways, he chose not to fight their battles.

Jesus expressed an anguished desire for something he chose not to sovereignly bring to pass:

Matthew 23:37 O Jerusalem, Jerusalem, thou that killest the prophets, and stonest them that are sent unto thee, how often would I have gathered your children together, even as a hen gathereth her chickens, and ye would not!

He mourned for his people knowing the awful price they would have to pay for rejecting him. Yet, he didn't change their hearts.

Psalm 78:41 Yea, they turned back and tested God, and limited the Holy One of Israel.

They limited the limitless God! We cannot comprehend God's disappointment and sorrow over his wayward children turning from him again. This scripture reveals his self-limitation in that he chose not to prevent their rebellion.

By the way, he won't prevent our rebellion either though it causes him great sadness.

Luke 12:50 But I have a baptism to be baptized with; and how am I constrained till it be accomplished!

Well, believer, he is no longer constrained! What a glorious baptism in the Holy Ghost he has given to empower his people to be true witnesses and to live holy lives acceptable unto him. If you have not yet received this glorious empowerment, I implore you to earnestly seek it. This baptism will overshadow any and all other experiences you have had in the Lord and will sustain you as you journey toward the glory world.

In your own life, be cautious that you do not limit the limitless God.

WHILE AARON WAS BUSY

After receiving lengthy detailed instruction from God upon Mt. Sinai concerning his laws, including the Ten Commandments, Tabernacle, Ark of the Covenant, government of the people, and the priestly function of Aaron and his four sons, Moses was informed of what God already knew.

Exodus 32:7-8 And the Lord said unto Moses, Go, get thee down; for thy people whom thou broughtest out of the land of Egypt, have corrupted themselves. They have turned aside quickly out of the way which I commanded them: they have made a melted calf, and have worshipped it and have sacrificed thereunto ...

It's interesting that God didn't say these were his people that he brought out of Egypt. He said, "thy people," and "whom thou broughtest." He also said that they had made a melted calf without mentioning that Aaron had made the melted calf. Interesting.

When Moses returned and saw the corruption of naked people dancing around the golden calf, his anger became rage. He broke the stone commandments on the ground and took the golden calf and burned it in the fire.

Exodus 32:21-22 And Moses said unto Aaron, What did this people unto thee, that thou hast brought so great a sin upon them? And Aaron said, Let not the anger of my lord burn: thou knowest that the people are

214

set on mischief.

Nothing like a little blame-shifting! But Moses' concern was always for the people. He truly had a heart for God.

All of **Exodus 28: and 29:** are devoted to God's desire for Aaron and his sons. While God was giving elaborate detail for their priestly garments, Aaron was busy directing to people to be naked and dance around the false god he had made. **(32:25).**

The Bible uses the term "Aaron and his sons" twenty-nine times and the term "sons of Aaron" thirty-two times.

The following scriptures demonstrate that God's plans prevailed though they were announced while Aaron was leading God's people into an accelerated debauchery; an actual descent into madness.

Exodus 29:44 ... I will sanctify also both <u>Aaron and his sons</u>, to minister to me in the priest's office.

Exodus 30:30 And thou shalt anoint <u>Aaron and his sons</u>, and consecrate them, that they may minister unto me in the priest's office.

Two of Aaron's four sons lived righteously and fulfilled the desire of God; whereas the other two didn't.

Proverbs 24:27 ... doth the crown endure to every generation?

It's been said that God doesn't have grandchildren. He does have praying moms, dads, and grandparents who call upon him continually.

This study was written to encourage you to look beyond the present reality to the broader overview of God. It could be that you have loved-ones who may be dancing naked around a golden calf even as you read these words. And it could also be that God is looking way ahead to his plans for their future.

Just remember that we have unlimited access to the Almighty God who reigns supreme. There's no telling what God will do in response to your intercession.

Made in the USA
Middletown, DE
07 February 2022

60731771R00126